BRIG

ZORBA THE GREEK BY NIKOS KAZANTZAKIS

Intelligent Education

INFLUENCE PUBLISHERS

Nashville, Tennessee

BRIGHT NOTES: Zorba the Greek

www.BrightNotes.com

No part of this publication may be used or reproduced in any manner whatsoever without written permission, except in the case of brief quotations in critical articles and reviews. For permissions, contact Influence Publishers http://www.influencepublishers.com.

ISBN: 978-1-645423-56-0 (Paperback)
ISBN: 978-1-645423-57-7 (eBook)

Published in accordance with the U.S. Copyright Office Orphan Works and Mass Digitization report of the register of copyrights, June 2015.

Originally published by Monarch Press.
Bonnie E. Nelson, 1974
2019 Edition published by Influence Publishers.

Interior design by Lapiz Digital Services. Cover Design by Thinkpen Designs.

Printed in the United States of America.

Library of Congress Cataloging-in-Publication Data forthcoming.
Names: Intelligent Education
Title: BRIGHT NOTES: Zorba the Greek
Subject: STU004000 STUDY AIDS / Book Notes

CONTENTS

INTRODUCTION TO NIKOS KAZANTZAKIS

LIFE, TIMES, AND THOUGHT OF NIKOS KAZANTZAKIS

Writing "Zorba." Nikos Kazantzakis (1883–1957) began writing "The Golden Legend of Alexi Zorba" during the great famine of

1941–1942. Due to lack of food, he spent many hours in bed trying to conserve energy. Then would come a knock on the door. If it was an elderly person, his wife would beg him not to open the door. If it was a child, he would give it a spoonful of oil and hastily close the door. 35,000 Greeks were dying of malnutrition, and Aegina where he lived was one of the islands hit hardest. Fifty-eight-year-old Kazantzakis believed that he was soon to die and asked his wife not to waste time worrying about the future. War planes, bullets, German land-vehicles, mass murders of unarmed civilians - these and more became part of his everyday existence. Although bullets shot into his house missed his head by less than half an inch, Kazantzakis continued to sit in the same place writing about the lively, lusty Zorba in order "to appease his hunger," as he put it. The full toll of this period of deprivation, however, was such that a doctor who later examined him asked if he had been imprisoned in a Nazi concentration camp.

Politics. During the famine in Aegina, Kazantzakis was willing to give up writing *Zorba the Greek* in order to join the Greek Partisans fighting in nearby mountains. Politically, however, he was unpopular with all sides. He knew that the Left did not consider him one of them and that the Right distrusted him for having flirted once with Communism. Still, he was quite taken aback when the Resistance leaders rejected his offered assistance, insinuating that he was a secret agent. In the same year, 1941, the National Theater refused, for political reasons, to produce a play he had translated. Referring to this play, Kazantzakis wrote his Cretan friend, Pandelis Prevelakis: "Apparently, there is no regime that can tolerate me - and very rightly so, since there is no regime that I can tolerate" (Helen Kazantzakis, 401).* Peter Bien, one of his critics and translators, maintains that Kazantzakis was abused by both Left and Right throughout his life because he was

---

* See "Bibliography" for full description of works cited.

too complicated: "Politics and paradox do not mix. Kazantzakis angered people because he seemed to embrace everything instead of defending one position consistently" (Politics of Twentieth-Century Novelists, 140).

Childhood In Crete. Born in 1883 in Heraklion Crete, Kazantzakis was the first of his family to pick up the pen instead of the sword. Until 1897 Crete had been ruled by foreign masters for seven centuries. And for seven centuries each generation of young men would - after siring the next generation - go off to fight for the freedom they prized so highly. The Turks who ruled Crete during Kazantzakis' youth were unusually fierce. In his spiritual autobiography, *Report to Greco*, Kazantzakis tells about a trip he and his father took one morning after the Turks had spent the night bloodletting. The tiny Kazantzakis saw fountains red with blood, and his father made him kiss the feet of two hanged victims - so that he would not forget. Captain Michalis, Kazantzakis' father, was renowned for bravery, and, like his father before him, became the subject of oft-repeated tales. All of his life Kazantzakis was in awe of his father, whom he writes about in the novel *Freedom or Death*. When the Turks rampaged outside their home, Captain Michalis assured his family that he would kill his own wife and children himself rather than let the Turks get them.

Stories of Cretan revolutionaries and his father's brand of heroism deeply impressed the young Nikos. He greatly admired the man of action, the revolutionary fighter, and was torn all his life between the life of action that he valued most highly and the life of contemplation for which he was more temperamentally suited. Again and again he belittles his writing or refers to himself as an "incurable pen pusher" or a nanny goat chewing "anemic paper." In *Report to Greco* he tells us that when he met

Zorba (the real man who inspired the novel), it was too late. He had already degenerated into the thing he "most scorned":

> **Would that I really could have turned those words into action! But I was afraid I could not. In me the fierce strength of my race had evaporated, my great-grandfather's pirate ship had sunk, action had degenerated into words, blood into ink; instead of holding a lance and waging war, I held a small penholder and wrote (443).**

This polarity of pen and sword, of contemplation and action, remained in Kazantzakis' personality throughout his life. Prevelakis likens him to a pirate who envies the ways of a Benedictine. Though he was not the man of action he would have liked to be, Kazantzakis was in many ways both the active, earthy Zorba and passive scholarly Boss of *Zorba the Greek*.

Education. No doubt the family wondered how Captain Michalis could produce such a "bloodless" scholar. Despite father and son's temperamental distance, however, Captain Michalis saw to it that Kazantzakis got the education he desired both from institutions and from travel. In 1906 Kazantzakis took his law degree from the University of Athens and went to Paris to study philosophy. In Paris he encountered the philosophy of Bergson and Nietzsche, who became his principal mentors. Bergson, one of his teachers, taught him about elan vital, the life force that can conquer matter; like Bergson, Kazantzakis was an anti-rationalist who dethrones reason and emphasizes the importance of the collaboration of intuition and reason. After his formal schooling, Kazantzakis spent five years traveling in Europe. Throughout his life he lived and traveled in Europe, Russia, Egypt, Palestine, China and Japan and was well known for his travelogues.

Nietzsche's Influence. Nietzsche's influence on Kazantzakis (especially evident in *Zorba the Greek*) was powerful and pervasive. In his youth Kazantzakis not only wrote a treatise on Fredrick Nietzsche and his Philosophy of Right, but he also took a "pilgrimage" to the towns in Germany where Nietzsche had lived. A few years later he translated into modern Greek, for an Athenian publisher, Nietzsche's Thus Spake Zarathustra. Later, in a chapter of *Report to Greco* entitled "Paris, Nietzsche the Great Martyr," Kazantzakis tells how Nietzsche helped him overcome his past education and traditional Christian beliefs: "Nietzsche taught me to distrust every optimistic theory."

I wanted whatever was most difficult, in other words most worthy of man.... Yes, that was what I wanted. Three cheers for Nietzsche, the murderer of God. He it was who gave me the courage to say, That is what I want! (338)

Even a cursory glance at Nietzsche's life and works reveals startling similarities to Kazantzakis' life and works. In their early childhood, each would avidly entertain audiences of family or servants by reading aloud stories about the lives of saints. Throughout their lives each harbored the dream of founding a colony of artistic, sensitive men. Both Nietzsche and Kazantzakis exalt struggle and "joy," which attends the strong man's efforts. Both emphasize man's potential to evolve higher. Both are nihilists and not infrequently make disparaging remarks about optimists, conventional people, and women. Two of their major works - *Report to Greco* and *Thus Spake Zarathustra* - are compared by critics. In important ways, however, they are dissimilar. Unlike Nietzsche, who continually made new discoveries and would contradict his own former views, Kazantzakis' ideas remained essentially the same throughout his life. Another dissimilarity is that Kazantzakis lacked Nietzsche's venom; despite his criticism of people who want secure, comfortable lives, Kazantzakis did not have Nietzsche's contempt for ordinary human beings whom Nietzsche characterized as "the bungled and botched." Nor are their views on God alike. While for Nietzsche, God is dead, for Kazantzakis there is a sense in which God may exist. (Textual analysis of Chapter 4 contains a discussion of Kazantzakis' concept of God.)

In describing the power of Nietzsche's influence, Prevelakis writes that in 1908, after Kazantzakis became familiar with Nietzsche's philosophy, "the great themes" which were to occupy Kazantzakis all his life - "optimistic or Dionysiac nihilism, the theory of the Superman, the bankruptcy of Western civilization" - became clear in his mind. According to Prevelakis, these Nietzschean ideas that the young Kazantzakis discussed in Fredrick Nietzsche and the Philosophy of Right remained substantially unchanged throughout his life.

Searching And Unsettled. In 1924, when Kazantzakis returned from the starvation and inflation of postwar Berlin, he had mastered five modern languages in addition to Latin and ancient and modern Greek. His translations included works of Bergson, Darwin, Eckermann, William James, Maeterlinck, Nietzsche, and Plato. His writings at this point included a novella, numerous verse plays, and his credo The Saviors of God: Spiritual Exercises (completed in 1923 and first published in 1928). In 1919 he had served briefly as Director General of the Ministry of Public Welfare in order to repatriate 15,000 Greeks from South Russia and the Caucasus. By this time he had also made two trips which later provided material for the novel Zorba the Greek. One was a trip to Mount Athos in Macedonia where he lived alone in a monk's cell for six months. The other in 1917 was a lignite mining adventure

6

in the Peloponnesus where he came to know Giorghos Zorba - the model for the fictional Zorba.

Despite all these accomplishments, Kazantzakis was still unsettled, still searching. He felt that Western civilization was bankrupt and that modern man was living in a void left by the downfall of Christianity: in *The Saviors of God: Spiritual Exercises* he says "an entire world is crashing down." In this void the old gods are dying, and the new gods have yet to be born. He personally felt that, in some way, he must help the new gods be born. In his university days he had written a play, "The Snake and Lily" (1906), which portrays victims who are trapped in the "transitional age" and can find no exit. In order to escape, the heroine of the play can only kill herself. For her there is not yet a new faith, a new myth which gives freedom from despair and frustration: "Our epoch is not a moment of equilibrium in which refinement, reconciliation, peace, and love might be fruitful virtues" (The Saviors of God: Spiritual Exercises, 114). According to Kazantzakis, man has the potentiality of fashioning a new god and a new world for himself. Because he thought this could be accomplished politically, he abandoned Christ and Buddha and fastened his hopes on Lenin and the Bolsheviks. But soon he was having misgivings about the "big ideas," especially the materialistic emphases. In 1928 after his fourth trip to Russia, he had become disillusioned with Communism for not fulfilling man's spiritual needs. However, despite civil wars, world wars and continual political disillusionment, Kazantzakis (like his friend Albert Schweitzer) spent his entire life attempting to understand and strengthen man's spiritual values. Repeatedly he says that his purpose is to "transubstantiate" flesh into spirit.

"The Odyssey: A Modern Sequel." During the time he was becoming disillusioned with Communism, Kazantzakis was discovering what he wanted to do. He - the **epic** poet - would provide a myth, a model for a new consciousness. From 1924 to 1928 Kazantzakis wrote and rewrote seven times his **epic** of 33,333 verses. First published in 1938, *Odyssey: A Modern Sequel* is considered by many critics to be "a monument of the age," one of the great literary events of our time. Kazantzakis begins exactly where Homer left off. Odysseus washes off the blood of Penelope's suitors. But having sheathed his sword, he finds Ithaca a bore. His wife, his son, his father, and his kingdom mean nothing to him now. Choosing five companions, he sets off again. He undergoes an incredible range of experiences, including stealing Helen from Menelaus and eventually losing all of his companions. Throughout his journeys he meets symbolic figures resembling Buddha, Don Quixote, Christ, the Primitive, the Hedonist. After seeing his newly-built ideal city destroyed by an earthquake, Odysseus becomes an ascetic, travels south in Africa, builds a small boat, and sails to his death on an ice cap in Antarctica.

God And Nihilism. Odysseus "the god-slayer" is Kazantzakis' new man, a synthesis of East and West, a model for how to live. Now that the God of the Bible is dead, Kazantzakis wants to replace the Christian-Platonic myth of salvation from the outside. In *The Saviors of God: Spiritual Exercises*, an important record of Kazantzakis' beliefs (hereafter referred to as Saviors of God), he tells us that there is not a God above and beyond man but a God who is in the process of being created by man. Echoing Bergson's elan vital and "creative evolution," Kazantzakis sees all life as a struggle of spirit to free itself from matter. (See textual analysis of Chapter 4 for further discussion of Bergson and Kazantzakis' concept of God.) From this struggling, evolving spirit, Kazantzakis takes his concept of God. Mud, plants, animals, men are ascending steps in God's upward struggle. For Kazantzakis, God is not almighty. God needs men, and special men who strive to liberate spirit from matter actually become "saviors of God": God "struggles for he is in peril every moment; he trembles and struggles in every living thing and he cries out" (Saviors of God, 103). It is man's duty - in whatever individual path he chooses - to help God, "to transubstantiate matter and turn it into spirit." There is no other discernible purpose or goal; for Kazantzakis freedom is not the goal but the process of struggle itself. The struggle is what matters, the struggle without fear or hope is what gives man his freedom.

This view - that there is no one path to salvation and no purpose to human struggle other than the struggle itself to liberate spirit from matter - is what many critics consider nihilism or pessimism; they variously label Kazantzakis' world view as "nihilism of the first order," "Dionysiac nihilism," "thorough-going pessimism," "heroic pessimism," etc. (See Textual Analysis for further discussion of Kazantzakis' world view.) Kimon Friar, translator of The Odyssey: A Modern Sequel, is more impressed with Kazantzakis' affirmation of life, "his great Yes," rather than his nihilistic despair, "his great No." However, Pandelis Prevelakis - a much older friend of Kazantzakis - points out that Friar knew only the older Kazantzakis, not the younger Kazantzakis" at the height of his nihilistic struggles."

Novels And Acclaim. Soon after his The Odyssey: A Modern Sequel was published (1938) came the Second World War and then the Greek Civil War. Although he served briefly as Minister of National Education (1945), Kazantzakis despaired of the political and religious situation in Greece. Leaving Greece in 1948, he settled for the remaining years of his life in Antibes on the French Riviera. Except for a brief time as Director of the United Nations Economic, Social, and Cultural Organization (UNESCO), Bureau of Translations, he spent most of his time writing novels.

Kazantzakis had come late in life to novel writing. His first novel, Freedom or Death, was begun in 1936, Zorba the Greek was written in 1942, The Greek Passion in 1948, The Last

Temptation of Christ in 1951, and Saint Francis in 1953. In 1953, when Kazantzakis was 70 years old, he had been repeatedly nominated for the Nobel Prize and was known throughout Europe for his novels which had been translated into thirty languages. After years of non-recognition, however, Kazantzakis had to suffer an acclaim that gained him many detractors. Some readers and critics were especially incensed at his portrayals of Christ. *The Greek Passion* angered the Greek Orthodox Church, which threatened to ex-communicate him. Freedom or Death and *Zorba the Greek* angered many Greeks who took exception to his non-romanticized portrayal of Greek peasants, and *The Last Temptation of Christ* roused the ire of Greek, Roman Catholics, and Protestants alike. Perhaps the biggest fury of all was caused by his use of demotic Greek - the language of the peasants. For a long time Kazantzakis had been a partisan in the continuing Greek language controversy. Intellectuals thought that he should respect "pure" Greek and use only Atticistic Greek, while even the advocates of demotic Greek accused him of going too far in his use of obscure and vulgar words.

Personality. Throughout his life Kazantzakis had become accustomed to little recognition and little financial reward for his work. Just one example of his many publishing reversals is the fate of the first publication of *Zorba the Greek* in 1947. Three publishers had asked for it, and the one Kazantzakis gave it to went bankrupt the day the novel was reviewed. Later when another publisher tried to purchase the remaining copies of the book, Kazantzakis discovered that the novel had been secretly sold without his knowledge.

Kazantzakis was not writing for money or fame. Again and again he took the very position that would be the least popular. Again and again he refused to compromise his life-style for money and security. Solitude was of primary importance to him. He did not like cities and could usually be found in sparse quarters somewhere near the ocean. His way of life fostered the passionate closeness to nature that is evident in all his writing. Friends and acquaintances remarked on his simple life and inexhaustible capacity for work. In personal habits he was frequently compared to a monk. He insists that he wound up an "ascetic" only because he "preferred nakedness to the cheap, humiliating livery of the bourgeoisie." The simple life, however, Kazantzakis tells us in *Report to Greco*, may seem very complicated and subversive to ordinary people. Of his own personality, he said he possessed "the glance of the elephant," which Buddha recommended for his disciples:

See all things as if it were for the first time;
See all things as if it were for the last time!

Kimon Friar, his friend and translator, emphasizes the paradoxes and "tension between opposites" in Kazantzakis' nature. According to Friar, Kazantzakis was a gentle ascetic who passionately admired violent men of action like Zorba and Odysseus; he ate little but admired voracious eaters, was sensitive to women but frequently portrayed brash males, was childless but delighted in describing large families. Likewise, he had a deep love of Greece, especially Crete, but spent most of his life "expatriate," had compassion for mankind but found it difficult to like individual men, was indignant about injustices but believed cruelty and injustice were necessary parts of life (Introduction to *The Odyssey: A Modern Sequel*, page XXV).

Final Years. In 1953 Kazantzakis became ill with leukemia. This did not prevent his accepting an invitation in 1957 to visit China again. On the return trip he fell ill from a smallpox vaccination and complications which set in. Hospitalized in Freiburg, Germany, where his friend Albert Schweitzer visited him, Kazantzakis died on October 26, 1957. In Athens, Greeks made arrangements for a funeral befitting a national hero, but the Archbishop decreed that the heretic Kazantzakis could not lie in state in any church in Greece or Crete. Decree or not, 50,000 gathered at his birthplace in Crete for a funeral procession and Christian burial. In the procession students from the Academy of Heraklion carried copies of the more than thirty books of drama, philosophy, travel, poetry, and fiction written by Nikos Kazantzakis. When his coffin was to be lowered, a large Zorba-like man stepped out of the crowd. This captain and well-known guerrilla fighter directed his own men to lower the coffin: "Such a man as this," he rumbled, "must be put into his grave by heroes, not by men who serve at ordinary funerals" (Riley, 48).

As he had directed, Kazantzakis' tomb inscription reads:

I hope for nothing.
I fear nothing.
I am free.

ZORBA THE GREEK

. . . .

1883	Born February 18, in Heraklion, Crete (Dates for his birth and other events in his life vary from source to source. This date is given by Prevelakis and Helen Kazantzakis.)
1897–1899	Lived on Greek island of Naxos because of Cretan uprising against Turks
1906	Took law degree from University of Athens
1907–1909	Studied philosophy in Paris
1917	Lignite mining adventure on which many events in *Zorba the Greek* are based
1919	Director General in the Greek Ministry of Welfare
1922	In Vienna writing about Buddha Leaves for stay in Berlin

1924	First trip to the Soviet Union (Three other trips in 1925, 1927, and 1928)
1928	*The Saviors of God: Spiritual Exercises* (Salvatores Dei -philosophy) published
1933-1945	Lived on Greek Island, Aegina
1934	Toda Raba (novel written in French) published
1938	*The Odyssey: A Modern Sequel* (poetry) published
1945	Minister of National Education in Greece
1946	*Zorba the Greek* (novel) published Visited England on invitation from British Council
1947-1948	Director of UNESCO Bureau of Translations
1948-1957	Lived in Antibes on French Riviera
1951	*The Greek Passion* (novel) published
1952	*Zorba the Greek* (novel), English translation published in London (in United States, one year later)
1954	*The Greek Passion* (novel) and *Freedom and Death* (novel), English translations published
1955	*The Last Temptation of Christ* (novel) published
1957	Accepted an invitation to visit China Died October 26 in Freiburg, Germany

1958   *The Odyssey: A Modern Sequel* (poetry), English translation published

1960   The Saviors of God: Spiritual Exercises (philosophy) and *The Last Temptation of Christ* (novel), English translations published

1962   *Saint Francis* (novel), English translation published

1963   *The Rock Garden* (novel), *Japan, China* (nonfiction), and *Spain* (nonfiction), English translations published

1964   *Toda Raba* (novel written in French) and *The Fratricides* (novel), English translations published

1965   *Report to Greco* (nonfiction) and *Journey to the Morea* (nonfiction), English translations published

1966   *England: A Travel Journal* (nonfiction), English translation published

1969   *Three Plays* (drama), English translation published

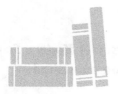

ZORBA THE GREEK

THEMES AND TECHNIQUES

. . . .

The preceding textual analysis has shown that major and minor themes recurring throughout the novel are presented through a variety of literary techniques. Themes, techniques, and relationship between themes and techniques are summarized in this section. For detailed discussions of specific topics, students should consult appropriate sections in the textual analysis.

THEMES

The first **theme** discussed might be considered the major theme to which all other **themes** in the novel are related. However, Kazantzakis' world view and fiction techniques make it difficult neatly to categorize or separate one **theme** from another. Readers should, therefore, be aware that many themes listed below are overlapping and interrelated.

1. Dualities In Human Experience: Body Versus Mind, Action Versus Contemplation. Like Bergson, Kazantzakis emphasizes life's dualities or polarities. Just as the

universe exhibits the opposition between descending matter and ascending spirit, so man's nature is a tension of opposites: flesh versus spirit, instinct versus reason, body versus mind, action versus contemplation, and so on. Half of these opposite characteristics dominate in Boss and the other half dominate in Zorba. Among many dualities in this novel are dancing and writing, Buddha and the shepherd, real and ideal, death and birth, night and day, light and dark, male and female, slavery and freedom, heaven and earth, man and God, socialism and capitalism.

2. Nature And Importance Of "Zorbatic" Or Dionysiac Qualities. Dionysus or Bacchus was the ancient Greek god of wine, instinct, suffering, passion, joy, drama, dance, and music. Demonic, primitive Zorba possesses the Dionysiac qualities which Kazantzakis (like Nietzsche) praises. Because he believes that Apollonian sobriety and order have dominated too long, Kazantzakis emphasizes the importance of "Zorbatic" - Dionysiac qualities and hopes for a civilization that will foster a genuine synthesis of Dionysus and Apollo.

3. Man And God In Process Of Evolution. Kazantzakis believes in evolution that will be creative evolution only if man struggles to free himself and "transubstantiate matter into spirit." (This is also Bergson's view in Creative Evolution.) According to this view - which exactly reverses the Judeo-Christian tradition - man is the creator and savior of God. (For detailed discussion of this **theme** see textual analysis of Chapters 2–5.)

4. Responsibility Of Creative Artists. The artist must record his impressions as honestly as possible in order to help

man evolve. Kazantzakis' brand of idealism emphasizes the creative potential of all men and especially the power of artists to create myths that aid future generations "to be born one drop more integrally." This, says Kazantzakis, is not a pastime but - given the state of our civilization - a "grave" duty. Boss fulfills this duty when he writes about Zorba. (For further discussion of this **theme** see textual analysis of Chapters 10 and 25. Also, see textual analysis of Chapters 8-9 for discussion of idealism.)

5. Bankruptcy Of Western Civilization. Old molds, gods, myths (especially the myth of salvation from the outside) are no longer adequate for modern man. Boss refers frequently to the need for new sources of meaning. This **theme** is closely related to theme 2 about Dionysus and theme 4 about the responsibility of creative artists. (See "Life, Times, and Thought of Nikos Kazantzakis" for further discussion of this theme.)

6. Search For Synthesis. Like Kazantzakis, Boss wants a synthesis of Dionysus and Apollo, of flesh and spirit, of heaven and earth, and so on. Many opposites or dualities are dramatized on all levels of action in this novel. (See **theme** 1 about dualities in human existence.) In a sense Zorba (body), who works in the lignite mine, and Boss (mind), who sits outside thinking and writing, are together a whole world, a synthesis. In most instances, however, the synthesis is a seldom attained ideal, which Boss achieves only in his manuscript on Zorba. (For further discussion of this **theme**, see textual analysis of Chapters 4 and 12-15.)

7. Women As Inferior: Marriage As A Trap. Throughout the novel women are usually characterized and discussed

as attractive but inferior creatures. Marriage and domesticity are considered for men a trap. See textual analysis of Chapter 7 for further discussion of this theme.

8. Nature Of Time. Time is explored seriously and humorously from many perspectives. Chronological or mechanical time is represented as only one measure of experience. (For further discussion of time, see textual analysis of Chapter 26.)

9. Limits Of Reason: Importance Of Man's Atavistic Roots. Although we walk upright and may prefer to think of ourselves as rational, Kazantzakis emphasizes the limits of reason and the evolution of man from animals. Throughout this novel, rational, logical, and legal behavior are often ridiculed and made to seem inadequate or inappropriate. Also, the inadequacy of words is frequently dramatized. (See textual analysis of Chapters 2–3 and 5 for further discussion of this theme.)

10. Buddha As Negator Of Life. Buddha denies the heart and retreats from life's contradictions by denying their existence. Throughout the novel, Buddha symbolizes a way of life that is inordinately seductive to people like Boss. (For further discussion of this **theme**, see textual analysis of Chapters 6 and 12–15.)

11. Hypocrisy Of Christianity. The Christian religion is depicted as a social form and myth from which spirit and meaning have long departed. Kazantzakis unmercifully exposes the degradation and hypocrisy of the monks living in a mountain-top monastery. (See Chapters 16–18 and 25 for further discussion of this theme.)

12. Power Of Dance And Music. Dance and music provide a de-individualizing experience that is much needed in the ego-oriented West. Like Zorba, dancers and musicians have a way of getting through the superficial surface of life to the primitive, chaotic center beneath.

13. Importance Of Myth And Imagination. Through myths and other uses of his imagination, man articulates his world view and illuminates his sources of value. If he is an artist, his recorded experiences may even help future men. This **theme** is closely related to theme 4 about the responsibility of creative artists. (See textual analysis of Chapters 10, 11, and 26 for further discussion of this theme.)

14. Resurrection And Rebirth. The meaning of resurrection and rebirth is explored from many perspectives. (For detailed discussion of this theme, see textual analysis of Chapter 21.)

15. Death And Reconciliation. The meaning and impact of death and the need for reconciliation are explored. The importance of understanding death's relation to life is emphasized. (See textual analysis of Chapters 22 and 23 for further discussion of this theme.)

16. "The Abyss": Responses To Nihilism. Because man fears the abyss - the "nothingness" of life, his responses are usually to deny the abyss' existence or to make up pretty stories like the one about going to heaven. Rare are the strong people, the Dionysiac nihilists, who can face the abyss and still affirm life. (For further discussion of this **theme**, see textual analysis of Chapter 6.)

17. Folly Versus Bourgeois Virtues. Folly is held up as an admirable quality while traditional virtues are frequently ridiculed. (See textual analysis for further discussion of this theme.)

18. Function Of Conceptions About The Ideal Society. Various conceptions of an ideal society are very briefly presented - not as an admirable political goal - but as something man enjoys thinking and day-dreaming about. (For further discussion of this **theme**, see "Life, Times, and Thought of Nikos Kazantzakis.")

LITERARY TECHNIQUES AND STYLE

Point-Of-View. Kazantzakis tells the story from Boss' point-of-view. Because Boss enjoys speculating about people's motives, he occasionally gives the reader information that he could not know about unless his point of view were the God-like, authoromniscient point-of-view. (See, for example, the information given by Boss in Chapter 19 about Dame Hortense's reasons for wanting to marry.) For the most part, however, Boss is strictly a first-person narrator who speculates, questions, and describes everything, especially Zorba. Because Zorba is such a dynamic contrast to Boss and almost seems to jump off the page with his dances and anecdotes, it is sometimes easy to forget that the novel is never told from his point-of-view. In order to achieve variety with only two main characters and still maintain a consistent first-person point-of-view, Kazantzakis has made use of (1) dialogue between Zorba and Boss, (2) anecdotes told by Boss and Zorba to each other, (3) letters and telegrams sent to Boss, (4) descriptions of the setting provided by Boss, (5) reminiscences and thoughts, which Boss experiences at great length (some critics say at "too great a length"), (6) dreams of

Boss and Zorba, (7) passages from books that Boss reads, and (8) extra-sensory perceptions when Boss gets psychic messages that his friends are dying.

Narrative Techniques. The novel gets slowly under way with a notable lack of surface plot and direct action. The characters move about in a "weather of myth" and - with the possible exception of Zorba - are two-dimensional, resembling characters in myth, fairy tale, and legend. The two main characters, Zorba and Boss, talk at length and tell many anecdotes. Despite the long conversations, episodic construction and initial lack of surface plot, the story becomes progressively animated with a fantastic energy, often expressed in gaiety or violence. Images and sensations abound and interweave with philosophical discussions that range from the bawdy to the profound. The time perspective is flexible; some of Boss' and Zorba's lengthy discussions take up days while the murder of the widow, the death of Dame Hortense, and collapse of the cableline occur successively in a relatively short time span. Despite what some critics have called "a virtually plotless tale," this novel goes forward with much important action on three levels: (1) nature (physical phenomena), (2) man, and (3) spirit and/ or imagination (especially as manifested in myth and legend). Frequently parallel action on all three levels focuses in the same image as in Chapter 10 with images of dark and light. (1) Level of nature: The dark days of winter pass; sunlight returns more each day. (2) Level of man: Boss welcomes daylight because of his disturbing night dreams about the widow. (3) Level of spirit and/or imagination: Candles and other lights are an integral and symbolic part of the villagers' Christmas and New Year celebrations. Action on all three levels may also parallel thematically as in Chapter 9 when struggle occurs in nature (the sun struggles to return), in man (Boss struggles to exorcise the widow), and myth (Christ struggles to be born). Always each level of action enhances or in some way affects action on another level. When Kazantzakis chooses to be blatant about the action parallels, the effect is usually very humorous - as in Chapter 21 when Boss makes love to the widow on Easter, the day of Christ's resurrection - or in Chapter 25 when the Holy Virgin of Revenge finally evens her score with Zorba and sits looking on as the massive cable and pulley system collapses.

Humor. Despite the philosophy and strange plot, this is a very funny novel. There is no doubt that the major source of the novel's humor is Zorba. His stories about his past are riotously funny, his tender-hilarious relationship-with "Bouboulina" is unforgettable, and his actions range from demonic to comic as he dramatizes the value of folly. Zorba is constantly myth-making and explaining his own version of how things happened. Despite his folly and bawdiness, Zorba has stature. We usually laugh with him not at him. In contrast, however, we do laugh at Boss, who frequently seems ridiculous in a way that Zorba never does. In comparison to Zorba, Boss' actions and words are humorous in a more subtle way. After Zorba, the next major source of humor is Kazantzakis' **satire** of the Greek Orthodox Christian Church in Chapters 16–18 and 25. Using **irony** - the satirist's favorite weapon - Kazantzakis introduces characters such as the mad monk and describes a monastery in which the monks' holy trinity turns out to be "money, pride, and young boys." Other sources of Kazantzakis' humor are: his Rabelaisian blending of bawdy and learned language, his choice of names for characters, his reversals of Christian doctrine, and his juxtaposing incongruous levels of action. (See textual analysis of Chapters 16–18 for detailed discussion of Kazantzakis' humor.)

Allusions. As a much traveled and learned man, Kazantzakis mastered five modern languages in addition to Latin and ancient and modern Greek. He also translated into modern

Greek works by Homer, Plato, Maeterlinck, Darwin, Nietzsche, Bergson, Eckermann, William James, and others. Thus, it is not surprising that his writings contain many **allusions** of a wide variety. There are **allusions** in *Zorba the Greek* to Shakespeare, Chaucer, Dante, Buddha, Homer, Marcus Aurelius, Sarah Bernhardt, Bergson, famous Greek wars, popular Greek songs, the Bible, the Koran, Nietzsche, and many more. Most of these **allusions** characterize Boss in some way. He reads Dante, and Mallarme as he tries to finish the manuscript on Buddha. He makes fun of Dame Hortense by likening her to Sarah Bernhardt and asking, "What Shakespeare was it sent you here amongst the barbarians?" In every chapter in order to explain what he means, he alludes to some aspect of Bergson's philosophy. Other **allusions** to Homer's *Odyssey*, Plato's "Myth of the Cave," Rembrandt's "Warrior," Nietzsche's "Last Man," etc., characterize Boss' quest to overcome his own inner divisions.

Description And **Diction**. Thoughts and sensations abound in this novel. Often the precision and quality of the **imagery** resemble those of poetry and have led some critics to acclaim *Zorba the Greek* as "a poet's novel." Frequently the same image (such as light and dark in Chapter 8) will occur simultaneously on three levels of action: in nature (sunlight returns more each day), in man (Boss welcomes daylight because of his nightmares), and in spirit or imagination (candle lights are used symbolically in Christmas celebrations). Using very sensual **imagery**, Kazantzakis describes at great length everything - thoughts, activities, landscapes, eating of food, and so on. When, for example, in Chapter 5, Zorba and Boss enter Uncle Anagnosti's home to eat "pig's balls," we are treated to rich descriptions of food, drink, weather, furnishings, even the castrated pig who comes by howling and looking angrily at the diners. Kazantzakis' liberal use of bawdy and earthy language is particularly appropriate for Zorba's personality. Boss' language - though less bawdy than Zorba's - is often sensuous. Occasionally he uses learned words, but, for the most part, even his philosophical language is straightforward and easily understood: "That's what liberty is, I thought. To have a passion, to amass pieces of gold and suddenly to throw the treasure to the four winds" (30). Kazantzakis' extraordinary love of concrete words led him to use demotic - the language of the peasants - instead of the "puristic" language of Athenian intellectuals. Translators have remarked that the flavor of demotic is lost in translation; attempts to accomplish the richness of demotic in English have produced instead a pompous, heavily adjectival prose.

Metaphor And Symbolism. The lignite mine - a symbol of action - is also the place where Zorba each day goes into "the bowels of the earth," which geographically and symbolically are the opposite of mountain tops where Boss has his psychic revelations. While Zorba (the body) works inside the mine, Boss (the mind) sits outside thinking and writing. Many other scenes, situations, and objects in the novel are symbolic. **Metaphors** too are in astonishing abundance due particularly to Kazantzakis' use of the richly metaphorical and concrete demotic Greek: "living heart," "large voracious mouth," "great brute soul" are some of the better-known **metaphors** used to describe Zorba. Particularly varied and interesting are the astonishing number of **metaphors** used by various characters to describe women. Many times the **metaphor** chosen is more of an insight into the character speaking than into the woman being described. For example, the widow, who "makes the steeples rock" for Zorba, is to others a "beast of prey," "a devourer of men," "a brood mare." And sex to Boss is an "obstacle," but to Zorba it is "the key to paradise."

Style And **Syntax**. Kazantzakis' **diction**, poetic **imagery**, figures of speech, flexible **syntax**, grammatical looseness, love of words for their own sake - all these stylistic ingredients, which are significantly influenced by his use of demotic Greek, are mostly lost in English translations. However, according to translator Peter Bien, demotic's heavy reliance on **metaphor** can often be conveyed in English. Certainly enough of Kazantzakis' original style is translatable since many readers of the English editions respond to the poetic qualities in the prose. Even when expressing Boss' or his own philosophy, Kazantzakis often manages to fulfill Nietzsche's dicta on style: everything abstract should be said in the most concrete manner possible, "every problem transposed to the level of sense, to the point of passion." Thus, for example, Kazantzakis' God "leaves bloody foot prints," and Boss says things like "The tiger was within me and he was roaring." Another important aspect of Kazantzakis' style is the shifting of images, themes, thoughts, and symbols from one meaning to another as he explores ideas, portrays characters, presents the setting, and builds up a tension of opposition between spirit and flesh, reason and passion, life and death, and so on. In these tensions and dualities, style and **theme** relate intimately. (See the discussion of **theme** 1 and "Dualities and Tensions Between Opposites" in textual analysis of Chapters 12–15.)

ZORBA THE GREEK

. . . .

CHAPTER 1

While waiting for a boat to Crete the narrator meets Zorba, whom he hires as foreman of a lignite mine.

Exposition. In the first chapter, Kazantzakis skillfully captures our attention in that part of the story known, technically, as the exposition (background information on characters, setting, and situation). In the first sentence of this novel, the narrator announces that he first met "him" in Piraeus and then leaves us wondering for some time about who "he" is. This atmosphere of expectation is extended to include everyone inside a Greek cafe at dawn: while we are waiting for "him" - Zorba - to appear, fishermen are waiting for the storm to cease, a sailor is waiting for a captain, the narrator is waiting to depart, even the fish are waiting to surface. In the meantime we learn about the narrator, whose consciousness focuses back and forth between reminiscences and the activities inside the cafe.

Contrasting Characters. Kazantzakis characterizes Zorba and the narrator as such polar opposites that sometimes they seem to be halves of the same psyche. In this chapter, a boisterous, animal Zorba drinks rum and tells stories of his much-traveled and experienced life. He has many names and his one prized possession is a santuri (a stringed musical instrument... a variety of cimbalom or dulcimer, usually played with a small hammer or plectrum). In contrast the quiet, intellectual narrator drinks sage and reminisces about one close friendship with a man named Stavridaki. The narrator has no name except "Boss," the name given to him by Zorba, and his prized possessions are manuscripts and books. Thus, sage and a book by Dante, rum and a santuri are symbolic of these two differing personalities who set out for Crete to work a lignite mine owned by Boss.

Symbols And Metaphors. A book and a musical instrument, as we have noted, can become symbols (a material thing or physical situation that stands for a nonmaterial thing or situation). In this chapter the most important symbol is an act: Boss' hiring of Zorba as overseer for his lignite mine is symbolic of his attempts to extend his personality and to experience more of life's "Zorbatic" elements. Here the lignite mine is a symbol of action. In descriptions of Zorba, Kazantzakis frequently uses **similes** (figures of speech that make an overt comparison by means of an "equal sign" such as like or as); for example, "He looks like a sailor." Typical of his metaphors (figures of speech in which comparison is made implicitly, without an equal sign), and one that critics frequently refer to, is Boss' description of Zorba as "the man I had sought so long in vain. A living heart, a large voracious mouth, and a great brute soul, not yet severed from mother earth." Another **metaphor** in this chapter is "This world's a life sentence."

Demotic Greek And Kazantzakis' Style. Kazantzakis chose to write his novels in demotic - the language of peasants - instead of "puristic" Greek used by Athenian intellectuals.

Demotic relies heavily on **metaphor** and has an unusually rich vocabulary, loose grammar, and flexible **syntax**. And, says Kazantzakis, this language is proof of a Greek imagination, "fiery and magnificent and tender." According to translator Peter Bien, only demotic's reliance on **metaphor** can be conveyed in English. In an "Epilogue" to another novel by Kazantzakis (The Last Temptation of Christ), Bien explains that demotic "always prefers the concrete to the abstract: the sun does not 'hang' in the sky, it 'tolls the hours'...; a camel does not 'get up,' it 'demolishes its foundations.'" Although awkwardness may result from attempts to suggest demotic **metaphors** in English, Bien asserts that "this is but a small price to pay." Throughout *Zorba the Greek*, thoughts, sensations, emotions, activities, landscapes - everything is described concretely with an abundance of sensuous **imagery**. Notice especially how frequent and detailed are descriptions of eating.

Philosophical And Religious Discussions. On every level - from the lowest "drugstore philosophy" to subtle, esoteric distinctions - questions and answers about the nature of time, freedom, duty, reason, soul, man, God, and salvation are bantered about in this first chapter. There's a reference to mud in men's souls, and a captain's reference to God's intervening in his behalf during a storm. After recalling his friend's views on duty and salvation, Boss rejoices in his freedom to open his Dante and immerse himself in either heaven, hell, or purgatory. In a more bawdy vein, Zorba defines reason as "the backside of the Miller's wife," and Captain Lemoni admits what he really thought when he saw the archangel of death. Thus in every chapter and on every level from the bawdy to the profound, Kazantzakis provides abundant evidence that this novel is not only about Zorba and Boss but also about art, nature, man, God, the meaning of life, to name a few topics considered.

CHAPTERS 2-3

Boss and Zorba sail for Crete. On arrival the two meet some local peasants and decide to find lodging in a rundown hotel owned by Dame Hortense. Zorba courts Hortense his "Bouboulina" with immediate success.

Dialogue Of Buddha And The Shepherd. In Chapter 2 the contrast between Boss and Zorba is heightened. Boss assumes qualities associated with renunciation and Buddhist compassion while Zorba assumes qualities associated with passion, with all that is the opposite of renunciation and Buddha. This same contrast is found in *The Dialogue of Buddha and the Shepherd*, which Boss reads before falling asleep. At the beginning of Chapter 2 Boss declares that he is in his Buddhist mood and that he feels compassion for men who do not realize that everything is a "phantasmagoria of nothingness." As Boss speaks, the real world becomes hazy until - suddenly - the mist lifts and Boss sees Zorba sniffing or scratching and making some pithy remark like "old junk!" or "fiddle faddle!" Chapter 2 - despite a consistent point-of-view -alternates between two very different moods and men. Topics of conversation - liberty, sex, folly, war, knowledge - change their meaning as they become first part of Boss' language and then part of Zorba's language: for example, sex is to Boss an "obstacle" and to Zorba the "key to paradise."

Point-Of-View. Every chapter of the novel is told from Boss' point-of-view. Throughout, the reader may not feel, see, hear, smell, taste or otherwise experience anything that does not happen in Boss' presence. Because Boss enjoys speculating about people's motives, he occasionally gives information that he could not know about unless his point of view were the God-like author - omniscient point-of-view. (See, for example, the information given by Boss in Chapter 19 about Dame Hortense's reasons for wanting to marry.) For the most part, however, Boss is strictly a first-person narrator who speculates, questions, and describes everything, especially Zorba. Because Zorba is such a dynamic contrast to Boss and almost seems to jump off the page with his dances and anecdotes, it is sometimes easy to forget that the novel is never told from his point of view. However, since Zorba is described often and since he speaks at great length to Boss, the reader is able to form an independent opinion of what Zorba is like. In order to achieve variety with only two main characters and still maintain a consistent first-person point-of-view, Kazantzakis has made use of (1) dialogue between Zorba and Boss, (2) anecdotes told by Boss and Zorba to each other, (3) letters and telegrams sent to Boss, (4) descriptions of the setting provided by Boss, (5) reminiscences and thoughts, which Boss experiences at great length (some critics say at "too great a length"), (6) dreams of Zorba and Boss, (7) passages from books that Boss reads, (8) extra-sensory perceptions when Boss gets psychic messages that his friend - and later Zorba - is dying.

Dialogue Structure. Chapter 2 has a dialogue structure with two very different speakers. One consequence of this structure is that many questions are asked and few are answered. Boss never seems to confront the question or problem being discussed. His responses - in contrast to Zorba's marvelous anecdotes - are frequently tentative and meandering. To Zorba's question of why men can't simply be good rather than both good and evil, Boss first makes a remark about it all being necessary, and then admits that he doesn't know the answer. Zorba - who faces questions head on - doesn't know the answer either, but he lives more easily with the contradictions and paradoxes of life than Boss does. Zorba is not a divided personality. Boss, in contrast, swings back and forth from admiring Buddha to admiring Zorba, from being a capitalist to being a socialist, from teaching Zorba to being Zorba's pupil, from pushing a pen to admiring the man of action. When Boss does make a definite statement or attempt a hale-fellow-well-met remark, he usually sounds like a child who is play-acting. "Chin up, Zorba," he says at a time when, despite Zorba's sea sickness, it is obvious to the reader that the otherwise sturdy Zorba hardly needs such coaching from his "misty" companion. Or, when they approach the Cretan village, Boss, having abandoned his Buddha mood, warns Zorba that the villagers "mustn't get wind of us: We'll act like serious businessmen. I'm the manager and you're the foreman"(33).

Setting. Kazantzakis describes superbly the sea voyage and Cretan landscape. Through the eyes of Boss, the reader is introduced to the countryside and peasants, whom Kazantzakis never ceased to admire.

Lack Of "Action." By now the reader has ample evidence that this novel constantly meanders along philosophical paths and has little direct, surface action. Most of the time we are either listening to an anecdote or following one of Boss' thoughts as he attempts to figure things out, to heal his self-division. Boss' language is surprisingly concrete, considering that he is sitting in the shadow of Zorba and talking about abstract matters. There is also a very subtle plot to each of his attempts to think things through. For example, he initially defines liberty in a definite, concrete way: "To have a passion, to amass pieces of gold and suddenly to conquer one's passion and throw the treasure to the winds" (30). But immediately in typical Boss fashion, he starts rethinking, rephrasing the question, arriving at conflicting answers, and finally dropping the whole matter for awhile.

Evolution And Transformation. The evolution of man and matter to something higher and the transformation of one thing into another thing are two closely related ideas that are important to Kazantzakis' philosophy. Chapter 3 contains important examples of evolution and transformation: (1) Sitting alone before dinner Boss feels "obscure" voices within that are "waiting to be delivered by me." Like Kazantzakis, Boss feels that he is a composite of all his ancestors as well as a means to the evolution of a higher being. He feels both "voices" from the past (his atavistic roots) and "voices" of the future (what man may yet become). (2) Boss believes that by communing with the soul of a poet, man's slavery may be "transformed" into freedom. (3) As Zorba's and Boss' food "changes to blood" both the world and dumpy old Dame Hortense become beautiful. Kazantzakis frequently uses the word "transubstantiation" - the process of changing into another substance. Transubstantiation also means (according to the doctrine especially of the Roman Catholic Church) the change of communion bread and wine into the body and blood of Christ.

With a little wine, women, and song the edges of the world should glow, of course, but Kazantzakis is also referring to the possibility of one thing becoming another through evolution, transformation, or a dialectical process whereby two opposites merge and become something else. Evolution and other processes of change are present in this chapter in outline but will come up again and again as the novel progresses. The reader should notice how frequently Boss juxtaposes, for example, flesh and spirit and ponders how flesh can become spirit, or how flesh can merge with spirit, or how spirit may evolve out of flesh, or how flesh may be transubstantiated into spirit. These four verbs ("become," "merge with," "evolve," and "transubstantiate") are very important to Kazantzakis because, for him, life is always a process.

CHAPTER 4

While Zorba directs work in the mine, Boss spends the day in their camp hut. After discussing men, women, God, socialism, etc., with Zorba, Boss declares his determination to "escape Buddha."

The "Whole Zorbatic World." Again and again Zorba is identified with the earth, nature, passion, primitive origins, "pristine freshness." In this chapter Zorba is characterized (1) by his own statements, particularly about belief in nothing except Zorba, (2) by his mining activities from which he emerges "out of the bowels of the earth" each day, and (3) by his effect on Boss, who, at the end of this chapter, very deliberately announces his intentions to escape Buddha and be more like Zorba - if possible. (For several interpretations of Zorba's primitiveness and effect on Boss, consult the discussion of "Dionysiac Zorba" in the textual analysis of Chapter 6.)

Kazantzakis' And Bergson's Concept Of God. Boss frequently alludes to some religious topic such as salvation, body and soul, death and rebirth, "the terrible struggle," "turning matter into spirit," "the hand of God," etc. From his reminiscences and remarks scattered throughout the novel, it is evident that Boss' concept of God is also Kazantzakis' concept of God, which - not incidentally - is also Bergson's concept of God. Anyone who wishes to understand Kazantzakis must understand his concept of God since "the major and almost the only **theme** of all my work is the struggle of man with God" (Helen Kazantzakis, 507). However, "God" to Kazantzakis frequently means the opposite of what "God" means in the Judeo-Christian tradition. "There is no salvation...," says Boss in Chapter 4; "supposing it's only when we obey [God] we are free? Supposing the word 'God' didn't have the convenient meaning the masses give it?" (57).

An important record of Kazantzakis' beliefs is Saviors of God. In this book he tells us that there is not a God above and beyond man but a God who is in the process of being created. Like Bergson, Kazantzakis believes life (in opposition to matter) is unceasing energy (elan vital) and ascent ("creative evolution"). Echoing Bergson's elan vital and "creative evolution," Kazantzakis sees all life as a struggle of spirit to free itself from matter. From this struggling, evolving spirit, Kazantzakis takes his concept of God: Mud, plants, animals, men are ascending steps in God's upward struggle. Or in Bergson's words in Creative Evolution:

The animal takes its stand on the plant, man bestrides animality, and the whole of humanity, in space and in time, is one immense army galloping beside and before and behind us in an overwhelming charge able to bear down every resistance and to clear many obstacles, perhaps even death.

"My God is not almighty," says Kazantzakis. "He struggles for he is in peril every moment; he trembles and stumbles in every living thing and he cries out" (Saviors of God). His feet are "heavy and blood spattered." He needs men, and special men who strive to liberate "spirit from matter" may actually become "saviors of God." This is also the God of Bergson's Creative Evolution. God "has nothing of the ready-made," says Bergson. "He is unceasing life, action, freedom. Creation, so conceived, is not a mystery; we experience it in ourselves when we act freely."

"The Invisible," "Cry," "Great Combatant," "Bull," "Crimson Line Ascending," and "Blue Bird with red talons" - some of the names by which Kazantzakis called God - could alone explain the furor with which many Christians denounced "that heretic, Kazantzakis." The anger elicited from traditional people did not surprise Kazantzakis since his views on God and on man's relation to God were in many ways exactly reversing the Judeo-Christian tradition. In Saviors of God and in all other writings by Kazantzakis, man is the creator who creates God. Belief in this God requires a new morality and duty: "It is not God who will save us - it is we who will save God by battling, by creating, and by transmuting matter into spirit" (Saviors of God, 106). God is everywhere imprisoned in matter and unless men free him, neither God nor man will evolve. Man cannot fulfill this duty, well-fed, in comfortable homes. Women and domestic life especially will distract man from his purpose. Kazantzakis emphasizes that God is created not out of happiness or glory "but out of shame and hunger and tears." Belief in this God requires a special "profound nobility" because there is no certainty of reward, no instruction, no savior, and "no road exists to be opened." Each man, says Kazantzakis, must find his own path of virtue or path of evil.

What is the goal of man and God? Where is this creative evolution going? Kazantzakis' answer is in essence - I don't know, you don't know ("The essence of our God is obscure"), but find your path and keep striving because it is your duty to struggle. And in the struggle without hope and fear is your freedom: "For life is not a goal; it is also an instrument" (Saviors of God, 115).

Emphasis On Intuition. In statements such as the preceding, Kazantzakis provides not logical answers but imaginative assertions about God and man. Like Bergson and Nietzsche (whom many philosophers consider more poetic than philosophic), Kazantzakis is intuitive rather than logical. He doesn't shy from asserting one thing as well as its opposite: there is salvation, and there is no salvation, for example. Or, he sometimes emphasizes the individual's will and efforts to find his own path, and at other times he says man should not try "to interpret or cast light" on God's rhythm but should adjust his own rhythm to God's. Because he wants both earth and heaven, spirit and flesh, he is at all times looking for "the synthesis." He wants (to use Boss' words) "a synthesis in which irreducible opposites would fraternize," in which he would win "both the earthly life and the kingdom of the skies," these aspirations voiced by Boss in Chapter 4 of *Zorba the Greek* are also Kazantzakis' aspirations.

Perhaps the least logical and most contradictory of Kazantzakis' assertions is found at the end of Saviors of God where Kazantzakis (1) first blesses those who say to God, "only you and I exist"; (2) then blesses those who say to God, "You and I are one"; and (3) concludes that "thrice blessed" are those who can bear "this great, sublime, and terrifying secret: That Even This One Does Not Exist!" In response to this passage several critics complain that Kazantzakis first asks you to believe in a certain view of God and man but then concludes by pushing it all into the abyss and saying there is nothing. Colin Wilson uses this final statement of Saviors of God as one of the "best examples in all philosophy of what logical positivists call 'nonsense,' a statement that invalidates itself by destroying its own meaning." Wilson finds this "taint of nonsense" in all of Kazantzakis' writing but concludes that Kazantzakis "is too big and impressive to be invalidated by it." Prevelakis reminds us that Saviors of God is a mystical book, and like all mystics Kazantzakis is trying to express the inexpressible.

Perhaps the haiku which Kazantzakis chose to quote frequently is also the best definition of his God:

I said to the almond tree,
"Sister, speak to me of God."
And the almond tree blossomed.

(*Report to Greco*, 8)

37

CHAPTER 5

Boss and Zorba visit Uncle Anagnosti for dinner. Later that night, after he and Zorba have been discussing socialism, Boss starts writing madly on his Buddha manuscript.

Who Is The Narrator? (With few exceptions critics spell "Boss" with a capital "B"; in the English language translation of the novel, however, "Boss" is spelled with a small "b".) Many critics maintain that in two novels, *Zorba the Greek* and *The Rock Garden*, the narrators are thinly disguised versions of author Kazantzakis. Several critics, including Colin Wilson and Peter Bien, refer to the narrator of Zorba the Greek as Kazantzakis (or K) and not as Boss (the only name given the narrator throughout the novel). There are in fact striking similarities between Boss-the-narrator and Kazantzakis-the-author. Boss' interests in Buddha and admiration for the man of action, for example, might actually be part of a biography of Kazantzakis. In his spiritual autobiography Kazantzakis tells us of just such a conflict in himself and acknowledges as well the influence of a George Zorba with whom he mined lignite. Other striking similarities between Kazantzakis and Boss as portrayed in Chapter 4 are Boss' interest in socialism and his desire to find a synthesis of "irreducible opposites." Later in the novel, Boss' views on God and creative evolution are identical to Kazantzakis' views.

The reader however, should be wary of simply equating Boss with Kazantzakis. Writers are, after all, free to make their characters a composite of whomever and whatever they choose. For example, the "glance of the elephant" is an important characteristic that Kazantzakis tells us he possesses; in *Zorba the Greek*, however, it is Zorba (not Boss) who possesses the "glance of the elephant." (See first section in this Note for a definition of "glance of the elephant.")

Cretan Peasants. Even his severest critics admit that Kazantzakis can characterize superbly the Cretans and their way of life. Throughout *Zorba the Greek*, Kazantzakis portrays the strengths and limitations of various Cretan villagers without romanticizing or brutalizing them. In this chapter Zorba's and Boss' dinner with Uncle Anagnosti is hilarious, deplorable, but -above all - memorable.

Evolution And Atavism. When Boss tells us that a tiger is roaring within him, he is describing not only his mood at the time but also a concept important to Kazantzakis. Kazantzakis believes that all of us still contain within us experiences of earlier ancestors and earlier forms of life from which we have evolved: "When you rise up in anger, a great grandfather froths at your mouth" (Saviors of God, 70). Man today, says Kazantzakis, is a mixture of all his human and pre-human experiences; the parts of man's behavior that are throwbacks or reversions to earlier forms of human and pre-human behavior are man's atavistic roots. We walk upright and may prefer to think of ourselves as rational, but because we have evolved over the centuries, we still experience some of the feelings of cave men and grunting four-legged animals. In *Report to Greco*, Kazantzakis tells of feeling the primitive violence of early "man" in his veins so strongly that one night he found himself shaking his fists in the direction of a village and roaring, "I'll kill every one of you!" (For further discussion of this concept and its relation to Kazantzakis' philosophy, consult the discussion of Kazantzakis' and Bergson's concept of God in the textual analysis of Chapter 4.) Note how much emphasis Kazantzakis puts on the irrational in men's nature.

| CHAPTER 6

During their evening conversation, Boss admits to Zorba that the mining adventure is just a pretext; what he really wants is "to carry ideas into effect." Overjoyed at this news, Zorba dances wildly. Later Boss agrees to Zorba's far-fetched scheme for bringing trees down the mountain.

Nietzsche's Influence. *Zorba the Greek* shows evidence of Nietzsche's powerful influence on Kazantzakis. Brief comparisons and contrasts between Nietzsche's and Kazantzakis' views have already been made in this Note. However, in order to consider Nietzsche's influence in greater depth, it is now necessary to consider some Nietzschean **themes** and ideas - especially Nietzsche's views on Apollo, Dionysus, tragedy, and "the synthesis." Some of Nietzsche's ideas and **themes** will then be discussed in terms of Chapter 6 of *Zorba the Greek*.

Apollo, Dionysus, And *The Birth Of Tragedy*. In *The Birth of Tragedy Out of the Spirit of Music* Nietzsche discusses two major aspects of classical art - Apollonian and Dionysiac. The Apollonian virtues were discretion, moderation, and prudence. Apollo was god of painting, sculpture, epic poetry, god of peace, logical order, and aesthetic emotion. His calm feminine beauty was in stark contrast to the active and masculine power of Dionysus or Bacchus, the god of Wine, instinct, ecstatic emotion, and suffering. Dionysiac behavior is characterized by insanity and excess. In drama the satyr-dressed (half-man and half-goat) members of the chorus were followers of Dionysus - god of song, music, drama, and dance. Nietzsche's thesis is that before Euripides, the union of Apollo and Dionysus gave birth to tragedy. Tragic Greek art was an attainment that civilization has not repeated since.

Kazantzakis accepts completely Nietzsche's thesis and describes the union of Apollo and Dionysus as a friendship in which neither subdued the other. In the chapter on Nietzsche in *Report to Greco*, Kazantzakis summarizes Nietzsche's thesis about the birth of tragedy and emphasizes that Apollo was "entrenched in his individuation" while Dionysus "shatters individuation and seeks the oneness beneath all multiplicity." This contrast between individuation and oneness is also an important contrast that distinguishes Western and Eastern thought. According to Kazantzakis, Western man follows the "tradition of reason" while Eastern man is prodded by subconscious forces. Western man categorizes, divides, emphasizes the individual and the ego. Eastern man - whether through renunciation (Buddha) or through passion (Dionysus) - seeks to blend the ego into a dissolving oneness; both Eastern renunciation (Buddha) and Eastern orgiastic passion (Dionysus) are de-individualizing experiences.

Greek tragedy vanished, says Kazantzakis. "It was murdered by logical analysis." Socrates with his dialectics and "golden mean" finally killed what was left of "Apollonian sobriety and Dionysiac intoxication" (Report to Greco, 324). Both Kazantzakis and Nietzsche hope for the return of the Dionysiac element in life. Kazantzakis agrees with Nietzsche that developments in German music might cause one to hope that a "tragic civilization" would again exist; music, especially dance, is a way of breaking through the superficial surface of life to the primitive, contradictory center beneath. Dance and music provide a de-individualizing experience that is much needed in the ego-oriented West. Both Kazantzakis and Nietzsche voice the hope that Socrates might at long last learn to dance. Nietzsche says in The Birth of Tragedy:

Indeed, my friends, believe with me in this Dionysiac life and in the rebirth of tragedy! Socratic man has run his course; crown your heads with ivy, seize the

thyrsus, and do not be surprised if tiger and panther lie down and caress your feet! Dare to lead the life of tragic man, and you will be redeemed.

Dionysiac Nihilism. Kazantzakis is not simply a nihilist but a Dionysiac nihilist, that is, a tragic man, a blend of both Dionysus and Apollo. Like Nietzsche, he refuses the comforts of traditional religion. He believes that nothing exists except elan vital, a continually erupting energy (one aspect of which he identifies with God). Many consider Kazantzakis a thorough going nihilist. As proof they quote the "Nietzschean" ending (or, as some claim, the "nonsensical" ending) of Saviors of God where Kazantzakis blesses those who can bear "this great, sublime, and terrifying secret: That Even This One Does Not Exist!" (See textual analysis of Chapter 4 for background of this quotation.)

When a person dares to see life without rose-colored glasses and finally progresses to the realization that "even this one does not exist," he is, according to Kazantzakis, standing on the edge of the abyss. **Imagery** of standing or dancing near the abyss is important to Kazantzakis. Because the abyss fills people with fear they may "want Christ to load [the world] on his shoulders and transfer it to heaven," or they may become Buddhists and escape the problem by renouncing and denying life. (Buddha, says Kazantzakis, "blows and makes the world disappear.") But the strong man, the "tragic man" becomes neither a life-renouncing Buddhist nor a Christian with pretty stories. The truly heroic, strong, affirmative man - the Dionysiac nihilist - dances on the edge of the abyss. He knows that all roads lead to the abyss, that all "answers" and beliefs are illusory. He (like Buddha) is a nihilist because of what he knows, but (unlike Buddha) his actions are an affirmation of life despite what he knows. Unlike Buddha, who negates life, Dionysus affirms life and therefore suffers. Because he suffers and struggles to keep going despite knowledge of the abyss, the Dionysiac nihilist experiences "tragic joy." Both Kazantzakis and Nietzsche praise the ecstasy and power of "tragic joy," which may be experienced only by the strong man.

The following parable (by the author of this Note) is a further illustration of the differing views of the Buddhist, Dionysiac nihilist, and Christian. Once three critics - a Buddhist, a Dionysiac nihilist, and a Christian - went to an outdoor drama titled Life as It Really Is! In response to the play the Buddhist said "No," the Dionysiac Nihilist said "Yes," and the Christian said, "Change the ending." The Christian wrote a long, wordy review for a syndicated column. The Dionysiac nihilist - without saying or writing a word - departed dancing. And despite severe weather, the Buddhist is still sitting in the open-air theater.

A Summary: Kazantzakis' Progression. In his childhood Kazantzakis was brought up as a Christian. As he matured, he concluded that Christ has thrown a veil over the annihilating abyss so that man would be comforted and protected from contradictions and nothingness. Kazantzakis did not want this type of comfort, so he turned toward Buddha and renunciation. Buddha could face the abyss without flinching. But Buddha was all intellect and little heart, and Kazantzakis could not accept this severing of heart and passion from life; he wanted to affirm - not negate - life. Like Nietzsche, Kazantzakis realized that Dionysus showed another way to face the abyss. Both Nietzsche and Kazantzakis exaggerate the importance of Dionysus because they feel that Apollonian elements have dominated life too long. However, both men insist that without restraint from Apollo, Dionysus is a monster. Thus, Nietzsche and Kazantzakis emphasize again and again the importance of the synthesis, the importance of the Dionysiac nihilist, who is a blend of Dionysus and Apollo, of East and West, of passion and reason, of serenity and ecstasy. As Kazantzakis says in Report to Greco (485):

> **Man very often lacks the persistence to maintain all of his humanity. He mutilates himself. Sometimes he wishes to be released from his soul, sometimes from his body. To enjoy both together seems a heavy sentence.**

Many critics insist that this synthesis is an ideal that Nietzsche never attained in his own life and that Kazantzakis only sometimes attained. Kazantzakis, however, did create a character, Odysseus, who is a Dionysiac nihilist. Odysseus, like all people who attain the Apollonian-Dionysiac synthesis, looks on life from a special perspective. This perspective Kazantzakis calls "the Cretan Glance."

The Cretan Glance. Kazantzakis wrote the following definition of the Cretan glance in a letter to a scholar who had accused him of being "anti-classical":

> **Crete, for me (and not, naturally, for all Cretans), is the synthesis which I always pursue, the synthesis of Greece and the Orient. I feel neither Europe in me nor a clear and distilled classical Greece; nor do I at all feel the anarchic chaos and the will-less perseverance of the Orient. I feel something else, a synthesis, a being that not only gazes on the abyss without disintegrating, but which, on the contrary, is filled with coherence, pride, and manliness by such a vision. This glance, which confronts life and death so bravely, I call Cretan.**

> **("Introduction" to The Odyssey:**
> **A Modern Sequel, XIX)**

Nietzschean Elements In "Zorba The Greek." The following list of Nietzschean ideas and **themes** found in Chapter 6 should give the reader a sense of the pervasiveness of Nietzsche's influence on Kazantzakis. The topics that Nietzsche discussed in his writings are italicized and are followed (after the colon) by examples of these topics found in Chapter 6 of *Zorba the Greek*.

(1) The Dionysiac Oneness Beneath Life's Surface: After reminiscing about his niece who once claimed she was growing horns, Boss exclaims, "What a miracle life is and how alike are all souls when they send their roots down deep and meet and are one."

(2) Influence of Food (Sometimes Nietzsche humorously would trace national character to certain foods; for example, rice makes a Buddhist; German beer is the source of German metaphysics, etc.): Zorba says, "Tell me what you eat, and I'll tell you who you are."

(3) Derogatory Remarks about Women and Marriage: "What can you expect from women?" asks Zorba. "That they'll go and get children by the first man who comes along. What can you expect of men? That they'll fall into the trap." Actually Zorba's remarks in this chapter are rather mild in comparison to remarks he makes about women in other chapters. (See textual analysis of Chapter 7 for Kazantzakis' and Zorba's attitudes toward women.)

(4) Inadequacy of Words (Bergson, as well as Nietzsche, complained of the inadequacy of words): Boss talks about inspiration being debased by words. Zorba complains of "mute bodies that only speak with their mouth. But what do you expect a mouth to say?"

(5)   Importance of Presenting Ideas in the most Concrete Manner Possible (The following is one of Nietzsche's remarks on style as quoted by Prevelakis: "Say the most abstract things in the most concrete and full-bodied manner... As far as possible, visible precise things, examples... No description; every problem transposed to the level of sense, to the point of passion"): Again and again Zorba's anecdotes fulfill Nietzsche's dicta about style. For example, in this chapter Zorba likens Boss' spiritual endeavors to a crow who tries to "strut about like a pigeon." Later, Zorba is ecstatic when Boss admits that his real purpose in Crete is not to mine lignite but "to carry ideas into effect." Typically, Boss has rather vague philosophical views on how to carry ideas into effect, but for Dionysiac Zorba "ideas into effect" immediately means ropes, cables, pylons, trees crashing down a mountainside, and so forth.

(6)   Importance of Dance: Overjoyed to learn that their mining is just a pretext, Zorba dances wildly because "My joy was choking me. I had to find some outlet. And what sort of outlet? Words? Pff!"

(7)   Our Ungrateful Age (the decline of Western civilization): Boss, realizing the importance of Zorba's folly and Dionysiac energy, concludes that "in our ungrateful age," Zorba must wander hungrily around like a wolf or else become "some pen-pusher's buffoon."

(8)   Importance of Revelry and Celebration: Zorba dances wildly. Boss celebrates his newly awakened senses and tells us of his pleasures. At mealtime Zorba returns to the hut bringing "all the things which rejoice the heart of man: clear laughter, the kind word, tasty dishes."

(9) Power and Importance of Myth: Boss tells of his youth when he "invented a myth, and the more I invented, the more I believed." (For further discussion of Myth, see textual analysis of Chapters 10–11.)

Dionysiac Zorba. Close scrutiny of each chapter would no doubt yield many Nietzschean elements and themes, especially in Chapter 25 when the cable-line collapses, and Boss dances ecstatically on the beach with Zorba. However, when considering the whole novel, critics generally agree that the outstanding example of Nietzsche's influence is the character of Zorba - his passion, folly, irrationality, dancing, acceptance of contradictions, impatience with bourgeois virtues. According to Joseph Blenkinsopp, "Zorba is pure Nietzsche":

> **Like Zarathustra, he walks like a dancer. To accept his invitation to dance is to risk a free fall into chaos over which we build our insecure catwalks of rationality and order. He is "a dangerous across, a dangerous on-the-way, a dangerous looking back, a dangerous shuddering and stopping" (*Thus Spoke Zarathustra*). He is Nietzschean man, above all, in his affirmation of life faced with the tragic absurdity of death.**

Peter Bien, who interprets the entire novel in Nietzschean terms, says (in *"Zorba the Greek*, Nietzsche and the Perennial Greek Predicament"*) that Zorba embodies "all the Dionysiac qualities elaborated in *The Birth of Tragedy*":

> **Passionate, irrational Zorba thinks only in terms of the present moment; he acts on instinct, not because he is an untamed savage, but because he possesses what Nietzsche terms "sheer exuberance,**

reckless health and power." Nor is his instinctive frenzy "a symptom of decay, disorder, overripeness" (Nietzsche). On the contrary, Zorba's impulsive excesses are meant to illustrate the Nietzschean dictum that "in all truly productive men instinct is the strong affirmative force and reason the dissuader and critic."

Andreas Poulakidas, who emphasizes the influence of another Nietzschean work ("Kazantzakis' *Zorba the Greek* and Nietzsche's *Thus Spoke Zarathustra*"), interprets Alexis Zorba and Boss, too, in terms of the "divided and diffused personality" of Zarathustra. The thin, wispy, bookish-looking Zarathustra goes about extolling a brash, sensuous, book-burning superman, says Poulakidas; Zarathustra's personality conflicts with Zarathustra's ideology. According to Poulakidas, Kazantzakis realized this conflict in Zarathustra and accordingly modeled Zorba on Zarathustra's theory and Boss on Zarathustra's personality. Thus, Zorba and Boss are "real entities that fulfill Nietzsche's Zarathustra both in philosophy and character."

CHAPTER 7

Boss asks Zorba about marriage and women. Zorba tells a series of chauvinistic stories about his colorful and intense relationships with women.

Zorba On Women. One critic suggests that on reading *Zorba the Greek*, a feminist might have "a falling fit." Without being an ardent feminist, any reader could easily find numerous "putdowns" of women in every chapter of this novel. Chapter 6 alone might dismay even a woman who thinks "a woman's place is in the home." The main source of chauvinistic remarks in the novel is Zorba. According to him marriage is "the Great Folly," and women are "the everlasting business." Women spend their time setting "traps" for men who are always big enough fools to fall into the trap. God really ought to have given men more sense, but since He didn't, men might as well enjoy "the hussies" whenever possible...after all, this is what women really want, says Zorba. Furthermore, "honest marriages" are "tasteless"; the "spice" is elsewhere. According to Zorba, woman is "weak," "incomprehensible," the source of great temporary pleasure, and because she's "not human," men should not "bear her any grudge." In one story about a Russian woman, Zorba says: "It was the time when roubles had become bits of paper. With a hundred drachmas you could buy a mule, with ten a woman" (95). During this time, he tells of meeting one of his favorite women, Noussa, who left him for a "handsome sailor." When Zorba concludes this story with the observation that he can't hold a grudge against Noussa because "woman is a creature with no strength," the reader knows that this conclusion is not justified from the facts Zorba has given about Noussa. She seems in many ways to be a female Zorba. Zorba, however, chooses not to value the strength or individuality of the women he has known but instead revels in his riotous, bloody, and sometimes tender memories of how these women pleased him. And yet, Zorba cannot be summarily dismissed as a loud-mouthed "male chauvinist pig." He is worried about aging and sings of his sexual conquests as a way of reminding himself of his powers. His stories about women are usually stories about Zorba's life force. In many ways - though it is no doubt difficult for female readers to view him this way - he is the innocent pagan reveling in woman as just another source of sensual pleasure. He does honestly like the women in his history. And since the story dramatizes how much "Bouboulina" likes him, the reader sees that Zorba does both give and receive pleasure.

Although Zorba's stories about women are usually funny, sometimes deplorable, and always interesting, what cloys are his remarks again, and again, and yet again in chapter after chapter about "poor women," "weak women," "the female of the species." Men of more sense just have to do their duty and make love to the "poor," "sighing" creatures. Throughout the novel, the similarity of Zorba's remarks about women's inferiority is enough to make the reader wonder if the problem is in translating Greek to English. Is it possible that Zorba's remarks (not his stories) about women are not so repetitious in Greek, that the Greek language has more misogynous terms than the English language? This might suggest a good research topic for someone interested in Greek.

Women As Characters And Symbols. Dame Hortense (Zorba's "Bouboulina") is the only woman in the novel who is developed to any degree, and even she possesses a two-dimensional, fairy-tale-like quality that is present in all of the novel's characters. With the possible exception of Zorba, Kazantzakis has chosen to present characters of this novel in a two-dimensional form; usually they function as types and symbols rather than as real human beings in three dimensions. At times, however, the portrayal of Dame Hortense approaches three dimensionality. When she is mourning her lost youth or showing delight in Zorba, she becomes more than a desperate old woman looking for a man, more than an aging prostitute seeking respectability. (Zorba calls her a battered old hulk looking for a final harbor.)

Of the female characters, only Dame Hortense is present for any length of time in the novel. All other females (including the widow) appear very briefly and function strictly as types and symbols. Even two female statues (discussed here as types of women) are as "real" as many of the "live" women. The lusty, musk-odored Widow Sourmelina - fuel for all male imaginations - is the village siren who lures men to their death. In stark contrast to the high-stepping, "brood mare" widow stands the rigid stone statue of the Holy Virgin; first as a symbol of mercy and later as a symbol of revenge, she is used by men for their non-procreative purposes. Another statue - the Tanagra figurine found by the Monk Demetrios - functions as a complex symbol both of what women may be and of what women seem in men's eyes to be: while Zorba sensually fingers the figurine's breast, Father Demetrios wonders about her monetary value, and Boss ponders her history as a goddess of fertility. Among other female types in the novel are: the rapacious mourners who steal from Dame Hortense; Crazy Katerina, who shrilly urges the men to avenge Pavli's death; and a Mother Superior, who calmly assures Boss about the nature of time. Also, there is Maroulia, Uncle Anagnosti's totally servile and mule-like wife, who never says a word and whose presence is felt only as a part of the atmosphere in Uncle Anagnosti's home. Among other women who are briefly seen but not heard, there are convent nuns, shy girls, and an old "hag" whose husband bitterly remembers her long-lost beauty.

The remaining members in this gallery of females are unseen, unheard, and are briefly present only as subjects of stories told by the men. (Because of Zorba's story-telling abilities, however, a few of these women are quite memorable.) Among these are Zorba's Grandmother (the foolish old woman), Zorba's daughter (the rebellious girl who eventually settles into respectability), actress Kotopouli (the professional woman), Boss' young niece (the wise child), Uncle Anagnosti's mother (the pregnant wife), another woman described by Uncle Anagnosti (the pregnant whore), Karajannis' African woman (the unfaithful lover), Karajannis' child (the malleable female child), a woman Boss meets in a sculpture garden (the intellectual woman), the "lady" in the story about The Fig Tree (the all-for-love romantic), and Noussa, Lola, Lyuba, Sophinka, the Bulgar woman, all of Zorba's many females (lovers and wives), who vary in character from fluffy pets to hard-nosed survivors.

After a listing of so many female types, it is important to stress that the major characters in this novel are men. Next in importance after Zorba and Boss is Dame Hortense. And despite this large gallery of female types, it is quite possible that twenty-four hours after reading this novel a person would remember only Dame Hortense and the Widow Sourmelina. This is not a comment upon the reader's memory but upon the fact that most of these women appear very briefly and function as part of the novel's atmosphere. A few like the widow - who is physically present for only a short time - are nonetheless very important to the novel's meaning.

Kazantzakis' Attitude Toward Women. Kazantzakis was a complicated genius with experiences and beliefs not easily labeled. He was both the man who chose fruitful relationships with sensitive, intelligent women and the man who filled *Zorba the Greek* and other works with ridiculous women and constant remarks about woman's inferiority. In his fiction and philosophy, man is spirit and woman is flesh; woman almost always equals sexual enticement and domesticity, both of which man must avoid if he is to evolve into a higher being and fulfill his purpose. Nowhere does Kazantzakis make this view of woman more clear than in his portrayal of Mary, mother of Jesus Christ, in *The Last Temptation of Christ*. While Jesus is discovering his mission and suffering many conflicts, Mary is upset because he is not like other men. She does not want to acknowledge that she is not a woman like other women. With the diminishing influence she has on Jesus, she tries to convince him that he is not chosen for anything higher than marriage and support of children.

It is difficult to reconcile the author who defines woman and domesticity as "the last temptation of Christ" with the author of this letter to his "Beloved Lenotschka":

And even when I create a good verse, there is someone inside me whistling and jeering and reminding me where I came forth, where I am going and there is no salvation. And only when I raise my eyes...and see you writing at the machine or doing the simple human household chores...only then am I consoled. The ephemeral moment suddenly assumes scope and the intensity of eternity. And I say to myself. For this moment which is so simple and human, perhaps it is worth being born and does not matter that one will die.

*(**Nikos Kazantzakis: A Biography Based on His Letters**, 238)*

This letter is part of a collection of letters, which attests to Kazantzakis' appreciation of many strong, intelligent women. This same collection, however, contains remarks such as this:

All the dark voices of the earth speak and command in woman's hot body. In man the spirit seeks an exodus, to get out of this beleaguered world, to be saved. And woman, divinely incarnating all the adverse powers, comes and stops him with her embrace (104).

However, in the "Epilogue" (written not long before he died) of *Report to Greco*, Kazantzakis says that throughout his life, he was fortunate in meeting "extraordinary" women. "No man ever did me so much good or aided my struggle so greatly as these women..." (413).

CHAPTERS 8-9

Zorba tries - without success - to interest Boss in courting the Widow Sourmelina, who fires the imaginations of the village men. As the winter sets in, Zorba and Boss discuss God and other philosophical-religious topics at length. Later, the reasons for Zorba's forebodings about safety in the mine tunnels are confirmed.

Dominant Images. Rain, the dominant image of Chapter 8, (1) triggers Boss' memories of his departed friends Stavridaki, (2) sets the mood for the entire chapter ("some sorrow...was rising from the damp earth"), and (3) operates on many levels as a symbol of sexual longing and fulfillment. ("The sky mingled with the earth in infinite tenderness.") Looking out at the rain, Boss experiences the "voluptuous enjoyment of sorrow," and in this appropriate mood and setting, he glimpses for the first time the Widow Sourmelina, passing by with damp hair and clothes clinging to her voluptuous body. The widow is called a "vamp," "fire," "brood mare," "mistress of the village" ("mistress" in the men's imagination, that is), etc. To Boss she represents a beast of prey, "a devourer of men," but for Zorba she "makes the steeples rock." The rain, the widow, the landscape...every page abounds with images that have the resonance and compact quality of poetry:

> It was raining. The mountain peaks were hidden. There was not a breath of wind. The pebbles gleamed. The lignite hill was smothered by the mist. It was as if the woman's face of the hill were shrouded in sorrow, as if she had fainted beneath the rain (107).

Passages such as this, no doubt, explain why *Zorba the Greek* is frequently called a poet's novel.

Idealism Of Kazantzakis And Bergson. Like Bergson, who wanted to free men from a mechanistic conception of life, Kazantzakis emphasizes man's powers to create his own world. In *Report to Greco* he tells us that "reality does not exist independent of man, complete and ready, it comes about with man's collaboration and is proportionate to man's worth."

In the very first sentence of *Saviors of God*, Kazantzakis is declaring this type of idealism when he says: "With clarity and quiet, I look upon the world and say: 'All that I see, hear taste, smell, and touch are the creations of my mind.'" Philosophically speaking, Bergson and Kazantzakis are idealists or epistemological idealists. Their kind of idealism identifies reality with perceptibility and denies the possibility of man's ever knowing anything about a concrete reality behind what the mind perceives. In other words, the appearance is the reality:

I do not know whether behind appearances there lives and moves a secret essence superior to me. Nor do I ask, I do not care. I create phenomena in swarms, and paint with a full palette a gigantic and gaudy curtain before the abyss. Do not say, "Draw the curtain that I may see the painting." The curtain is the painting.

(*Saviors of God*, 48)

Throughout *Zorba the Greek* are many passages referring to this idealism. In Chapter 8, for example, Boss says of Zorba, "He speaks and the world grows bigger." Or, Boss writes, "I have also collaborated in the work in which I am acting on God's stage." And much later, for example in Chapter 21, such idealism enhances the position of man-as-creator, especially man the myth-maker and poet who creates a vision of the world that is "truer than truth." To understand his idealism is to understand Kazantzakis' (and Boss') reason for writing. (See textual analysis of Chapter 26.) In *Report to Greco*, Kazantzakis tells us that poetic creation and writing may have been a game in times of equilibrium, but "Today it is a grave duty":

> **...if today's creative artist formulated his deepest inner presentiments with integrity, he would aid future man to be born one hour sooner, one drop more integrally.**
>
> **I kept divining the creator's responsibility with ever-increasing clarity. Reality, I said to myself, does not exist independent of man, completed and ready; it comes about with man's collaboration, and is proportionate to man's worth. If we open a riverbed by writing or acting, reality may flow into a course it would not have taken had we not intervened. We do not bear the full responsibility, naturally, but we do bear a great part (450).**

Zorba On God. Zorba describes God as "being exactly like me. Only bigger, stronger, crazier. And immortal into the bargain." This is perhaps the most quoted passage of the novel (121). Chances are that people who haven't read this novel will still know who pictures God as holding a large sponge and - "Flap! Slap!" - washing away sins. Unlike Boss' tortured musings about God, Zorba's views are refreshingly straightforward and anthropomorphic. Ultimately God is just a larger, immortal version of Zorba. After explaining to Boss his view of God, Zorba very much resembles his own God concept when he "miraculously" rescues his own workers from a collapsing mine tunnel.

CHAPTERS 10-11

Christmas and the darkest days of the year pass while Boss tries continually and unsuccessfully to forget the widow. He and Zorba riotously celebrate New Year's Day with Dame Hortense.

Structural Device: Levels Of Action. Throughout the novel, action occurs on three levels: (1) nature (physical phenomena), (2) man, and (3) spirit and/or imagination (especially as manifested in myth, legends, and religious rites). In Chapter 10 parallel action on all three levels is focused in the images of dark and light. (1) Level of nature: The dark days of winter pass; sunlight returns more each day. (2) Level of man: Boss welcomes daylight because of his disturbing night dreams about the widow. (3) Level of spirit and/or imagination: Candles and other lights are an integral and symbolic part of the villagers' Christmas and New Year celebrations. Each level of action enhances or in some way affects action on another level. In Chapter 9, for example, Zorba's fear that the mine is unsafe is intensified by a "primitive terror" that the sun might go out forever. In Chapter 10 the **theme** of struggle is intensified because struggle occurs simultaneously on all three levels of action: As light of the sun (1) struggles to return, Boss (2) struggles to exorcise the widow, and Christ (3) struggles to be born. While struggling, Boss consoles himself that he is not alone because "the light of day is also fighting"; the action parallels are sometimes developed more subtly than this.

When Kazantzakis chooses to be blatant about the parallels, the effect is usually very humorous - as (later, in Chapter 21) when Boss makes love to the widow on Easter, the day of Christ's resurrection - or (in Chapter 25) when the Holy virgin of Revenge finally evens her score with Zorba and sits looking on as the massive cable and pulley system collapses.

By juxtaposing action on these three levels, Kazantzakis is portraying the complex interrelationship of man's past, present and future...of man's physical self, psychological self, and spiritual self. In Chapters 8, 9, and 10 rain, dark, fear, subconscious forces are manifest in such a way that we understand the need for light, hope and celebration. Kazantzakis is here dramatizing both the sources of and the need for myth and legend. Watching the villagers celebrate the birth and hope of Christ, Boss pronounces what -in all of Kazantzakis' writings - is perhaps the best description of the author's view on the importance of myth and imagination.

Myth And Imagination. Boss muses thus:

If the scriptures had said: "Today, light is born," man's heart would not have leapt. The idea would not have become a legend and would not have conquered the world. They would merely have described a normal physical phenomenon and would not have fired our imagination - I mean our soul. But the light which is born in the dead of winter has become a child and the child has become God, and for twenty centuries our soul has suckled it...(132).

Notice above the emphasis on three levels as outlined in the previous discussion: (1) nature, (2) man, and (3) spirit or imagination. The above passage is also an excellent example of Kazantzakis' style - especially his use of physical images to describe the spiritual.

Themes Advanced. In these chapters we see further evidence (1) of Boss' inability to act, (2) of Boss and Kazantzakis' views on creative evolution, (3) of the Widow Sourmelina's influence, (4) of Zorba's "friendly accord" with the universe, and (5) of the tender-hilarious relationship between Zorba and Dame Hortense.

CHAPTERS 12-15

In these four chapters Zorba is away gathering materials. We see Boss alone as he reminisces (especially about Zorba), receives letters, travels the countryside, and defends the widow before the villagers who blame her for Pavli's drowning.

"The Last Man." Kazantzakis has borrowed this term, "the Last Man," from Nietzsche. In Chapter 12 Boss suddenly realizes that Buddha is the Last Man - the man who is all spirit and no flesh. ("This spirit has no soil left for its roots.") Buddha suddenly becomes for Boss the negation of life, the denial of soil, seed, blood and tears - a great destructive force, which Boss must struggle against. (See textual analysis of Chapter 6 for discussion of Buddha as the negation of life.) For his own salvation, Boss now feels he must hurry up and finish his manuscript on Buddha.

Dualities, Tension Between Opposites. As Boss struggles to be free of Buddha, all the dualities and tension between opposites in the novel are heightened and dramatized. (1) "The Last Man," Buddha, and Mallarme stand as negators of life against Zorba, the great affirmer of life. (2) Boss' intellect and rationalism are contrasted sharply with Zorba's zest and folly. (3) On the very same day Boss receives two letters - one about duty, love of Greece, etc., and the other about sensuous pleasure, hatred of Greece, etc. (4) Hopes for a life hereafter stand against Boss' increasing awareness of man's one life now on earth. (5) Soon after meeting a nun ("Immaculate Bride of Christ"), Boss encounters an old man who is bitter that his once beautiful bride has become such a hag. Other contrasts or tensions are suggested between (6) solitary - and communal life, (7) capitalism and socialism, (8) body and soul, (9) life and death, (10) virgins and mothers, (11) timelessness of eternity and seasons of earth.

CHAPTERS 16-18

After Zorba returns, he and Boss climb the mountain to rent a forest for Zorba's get-rich-quick scheme. On the mountain top they encounter a mad, pyromaniac monk, another monk who "likes" young boys, and many other characters who are part of Kazantzakis' broad **satire** on false knowledge, hypocrisy, and especially on organized religion.

Use Of Epithets. In Chapter 18 the unbalanced bishop who finds relief in listing the verbal adornments of the Virgin is meant to be a caricature of Kazantzakis himself. The delirious bishop closes his eyes and murmurs "Imperishable Rose, Fruitful Earth, Vine, Fountain" and so on. And no doubt, some of his critics thought that Kazantzakis himself was delirious in his zealous use of demotic Greek. Even advocates of demotic often criticized Kazantzakis for overdoing it, especially for using too many obscure words. (See textual analysis of Chapter 1 for a discussion of demotic Greek.) For example, in his **epic** poem, *The Odyssey: A Modern Sequel*, Kazantzakis used more than two-hundred different epithets to describe Odysseus.

Kazantzakis' Humor. Today humor is usually distinguished from wit - wit being more intellectual than humor, which implies some kind of sympathetic response to the human condition. What is the nature of this response? Why do we laugh, and why is the same thing not always funny? What is humor?

According to Aristotle, the causes of laughter are "errors and deformities that do not pain or injure us." Another philosopher, Thomas Hobbes, emphasizes "self-glory," the distance between the person laughing and the person or thing being laughed at. Henri Bergson, somewhat in Hobbes' vein, writes about social rigidities, mechanical actions, and laughter as a weapon of elan vital. While Herbert Spencer, Immanuel Kant, and Arthur Schopenhauer posit an "incongruity theory," Sigmund Freud suggests that laughter has to do with suppressed sexual or aggressive tendencies. Max Beerbohm very smilingly considers all theories of humor to be...well... laughable.

Without first subscribing to any one theory of humor, let us examine some of the humorous situations and sources of laughter in *Zorba the Greek*. There is no doubt that the major source of the novel's humor is Zorba. His stories about his past are riotously funny, his tender-hilarious relationship with "Bouboulina" is unforgettable, and his actions range from demonic to comic as he dramatizes the value of folly by taking his "brakes" off at just that point when most sensible people would put their "brakes" on. Even his casual remarks are colorful ("Life is trouble, yes... Death, no"). His questions, unlike Boss' philosophical and circuitous musings, cut immediately and humorously to the heart of a matter: "How do you expect to get the better of a devil, boss, if you don't turn into a devil-and-a-half yourself?" According to him, "daytime is a man," "night is a woman," money is "wings," God holds a big sponge and - "Flap, Slap" - wipes away sins. Zorba is constantly myth-making and explaining his own version of how things happened. One of his funniest myths is the story of how poor Zeus, attempting to satisfy all women who had to sleep alone, couldn't get a good night's sleep and died so horribly of exhaustion that Christ - his heir - immediately pronounced, "Beware of women!" Zorba, however, occasionally dreams of setting up his own Zeus Marriage Agency. And, despite his folly and bawdiness, Zorba has stature. We usually laugh with him, not at him. In contrast, however, we do laugh at Boss, who frequently seems ridiculous in a way that Zorba never does. In comparison to Zorba, Boss' actions and words are humorous in a more subtle way - as when Boss has the "heavy weight" of a butterfly on his conscience or when he stands "like a post" at the widow's gate thinking, "In another life, I'll behave better than this."

The structural device of paralleling different levels of action (discussed in Chapter 10) is another source of humor when Kazantzakis chooses blatantly to juxtapose the "high" with the "low," God's world with man's world. For example, Easter, the day of Christ's resurrection, is also the day of Boss' resurrection and deliverance, i.e., Boss finally makes love to the widow. In many ways - in addition to plot-level parallels - Kazantzakis humorously juxtapositions "high" with "low," formal with informal, learned language with bawdy language. One schizophrenic monk actually embodies a "high" and a "low" personality: sometimes (when he is not Christ) he is Zaharia, who is good and obedient; but other times the scoundrel Brother Joseph takes over and sensually indulges himself.

Among other sources of humor are names of people and places. Kazantzakis was no doubt smiling when he chose such names as "Modesty Cafe-and-Butcher's Shop," "The Widow Sourmelina," "Holy Virgin of Revenge," "Bouboulina," and so on.

Although *Zorba the Greek* is humorous from beginning to end, critics frequently single out Zorba's and Boss' visit to the monastery as the funniest portion of the novel. In the monastery chapters and later when the monks declare the miracle of the Holy Virgin of Revenge (Chapter 25), Kazantzakis satirizes the Greek Orthodox Christian Church specifically, but by implication, he is satirizing all organized, Christian religion. Satire is the ridicule of people, ideas, situations - usually for moral purposes. Whatever the period or **genre**, the common element of all **satire** is criticism, implying what should be rather than what is - hence the moral implications of **satire**, which is usually directed at social institutions or human foibles. In Chapters 17 and 18

Kazantzakis shows us a monastery in which the monks' Holy Trinity turns out to be "Money, Pride, and Young Boys!" But just the act of exposing these degraded monks indicates that Kazantzakis has a high opinion of man's potentialities and of what the church once meant. Or to use critic Walter Kerr's words, as he discusses why Watergate scandals haven't provided good subjects for **satire** (New York Times, December 30, 1973):

> **The satirist stands on his subjects' shoulders, which are admitted to be strong; he then beats his victim about the head and ears for allowing excess to corrupt his excellences. Something like that.**

A favorite device of the satirist is **irony**, a very general term referring to a contrast or conflict between what is stated and what is meant. There are various types of **irony** (definitions and terms vary from text to text) and various techniques for achieving **irony**, but always irony implies a double vision, a second perspective (at least) on what is being said and done. An example of a very simple type of **irony** is the statement from a speaker who says "How great!" and really means "How awful!" When Zorba says to Zaharia, "Good, for the All High!," we-the-reader know that Zorba is really expressing contempt for the "All High" and for Zaharia. In the two above examples the conflict or contrast is between what a character says and what a character means. **Irony**, however, is frequently more complex than this, depending on whether the conflict is between what a character says and what the author means, between what one character says and what you-the-reader-or-audience know to be true, between what you expect and what actually happens. And especially in Chapters 17 and 18 Kazantzakis has riotously managed some additional ironic perspectives; for example, the schizophrenic monk who is sometimes Brother Zaharia, sometimes the naughty Brother Joseph, and sometimes (when he moans in his sleep at night) Christ. Zaharia, who thinks Zorba is Canavaro, provides the reader with one view on the monastery and on the worship of "Our Lady of Revenge," who was formerly called "Our Lady of Mercy" until she miraculously lost her temper and murdered some insulting infidels. Another good example of **irony** is Boss' thoughts and initial reception by the monks. Boss approaches the isolated monastery thinking, "What a marvel! What solitude! What felicity!," only to have his reverie interrupted by clamorous monks demanding to know what's happening in the world: "Haven't you brought a newspaper?" Here the irony involves Boss' expectations and view of the monks as well as the reader's expectations and view of both Boss and the monks.

Throughout the reader is constantly reminded of discrepancies between the appearance and the reality of this monastery. Or, to use Boss' words, the reader sees the hypocrisy and emptiness of this social institution, which exists in form only and from which the spirit has fled: "I thought how, even in decay, an elevated rhythm in life preserves all its outward form, is impressive and full of nobility. The spirit departs but leaves its vast dwelling, which it has slowly evolved and which is as intricate as a sea shell" (231). Here again is evidence of Bergson's influence; Boss' observation of form and spirit. actually paraphrases one of Bergson's statements about humor, about the potentially comic element in all social institutions. According to Bergson, for any ceremony or social institution to become comic, "it is enough that our attention be fixed on the ceremonial element in it, and that we neglect its matter, as philosophers say, and think only of its form."

About Bergsonian elements in Kazantzakis' humor, little has been written. Critics, however, have claimed that Kazantzakis is writing in the tradition of Homer, Aristophanes, Plautus,

Boccaccio, Rabelais, Celine, Rousseau, Voltaire, and so on. The only term that critics use almost unanimously to describe Kazantzakis' humor is - "Rabelaisian." Perhaps Kazantzakis' most "Rabelaisian" characteristic is his blending of "high" with "low," holy with mundane, and especially learned language with bawdy and everyday language. Like Rabelais (1494–1553), Kazantzakis is exuberant in imagination, extravagant and even coarse in humor and **satire**, and a believer in expanding man's consciousness. "Gargantuan," an adjective meaning gigantic capacities, size, appetites, and powers, came into the English language from Rabelais' giant character portrayed in Gargantua and Pantagruel. In many ways, Zorba resembles both Gargantua and Panurge, Rabelais' character noted for elaborately executed pranks.

CHAPTERS 19–20

Zorba and Dame Hortense ("Bouboulina") become engaged. Afterwards, Boss listens at length to Zorba's stories about men, women, the stupidity of war and patriotism, and so on.

Themes And Techniques. With the engagement of Zorba and Dame Hortense, Kazantzakis continues his **satire** of social ceremonies. In these two chapters we also see further evidence (1) of Zorba as myth-maker, man of action, and comforter of women; (2) of Kazantzakis' and Bergson's brand of idealism (detailed discussion in textual analysis of Chapters 8–9); (3) of the contrast between Zorba as the whole man and Boss as the divided personality; (4) of women as weak creatures who must somehow trap men...preferably into marriage. Kazantzakis has great fun characterizing the aged, recently engaged Dame Hortense as she is walked home past "The Fig Tree of Our Young Lady and the widow's garden."

CHAPTER 21

Because Dame Hortense is ill, Zorba and Boss temporarily postpone their Easter dinner. Later, Boss goes to the widow.

Resurrection And Rebirth. Chapter 21 abounds with **themes** and symbols of resurrection and rebirth: flowers bloom, insects hum, Easter bells ring, colored Easter eggs are opened, Dame Hortense dreams of wedding dresses, villagers shout "Christ is reborn!," and Zorba and Boss prepare a beach celebration to make Dame Hortense feel young again. The most powerful rebirth and resurrection takes place in Boss, who finally goes to the widow. Afterwards, smelling of her and orange blossoms from her garden, he ceases philosophizing, and-in Zorba-like fashion - gives himself totally to his surroundings and his memories of the widow's bed. The beginning of Boss' new growth and cycle is symbolized by his finishing and binding up the Buddha manuscript. And, since an end is foreshadowed in all beginnings and death is present in all births, this chapter fittingly concludes with a doctor being summoned for the dying Hortense.

CHAPTERS 22-23

In Chapter 22 the villagers interrupt their Easter celebrations to witness and encourage the murder of the widow - for whom Zorba and Boss grieve. In Chapter 23 Dame Hortense's death is described in detail.

Death And Reconciliation. As symbols and **themes** of resurrection and rebirth diminish, symbols and **themes** of death increasingly dominate in these chapters. The mood and passions of Easter dancers turn suddenly from frenzied celebrations of rebirth and resurrection to frenzied cries of revenge: "Kill her! Kill her!" The dead widow is obviously a scapegoat. She also becomes part of a myth that Boss recalls for consolation! This myth about the relation between death and birth is called by Nietzsche "The Myth of Eternal Recurrence"; Boss' reflections as he watches the Easter dancers are actually a description of this myth:

Every minute death was dying and being reborn, just like life. For thousands of years young girls and boys have danced beneath the tender foliage of the trees in spring - beneath the poplars, firs, oaks, planes and slender palms - and they will go on dancing for thousands more years, their faces consumed with desire. Faces change, crumble, return to earth; but others rise to take their place. There is only one dancer, but he has a thousand masks. He is always twenty. He is always immortal (272).

The Myth of Eternal Recurrence provides a macrocosmic overview. Life looked at from such a perspective shows, if not complete stasis, then only the broadest outlines, risings and fallings, flowings and ebbings of various cycles. Death, considered so philosophically, becomes a phenomenon rather than a close-up human pain, a cycle rather than a stenching, maggot-filled body.

The power of these two evocative chapters, however, is that death is explored from many angles, including the philosophical as well as the odoriferous. Zorba, Boss, and the Cretan villagers are experiencing or responding to death. Scenes and characters are briefly but vividly sketched. After the widow's death, the idiot Mimiko's behavior dramatizes his grief; thus, for the first time the reader knows that Mimiko loved the widow. The dirge singers, Malamatenia and Auntie Lenio, embody rapaciousness and hovering vulture characteristics present in many people witnessing death. Because Kazantzakis is not only portraying but also satirizing some of our human responses to death, the dirge singers appall and amuse us at the same time. We also see how ineffectual and ridiculous are the elders' legalistic responses and attempts to itemize Dame Hortense's possessions. In contrast to Zorba's heartfelt and sensuously expressed grief, Boss' responses are unbelievably cerebral as when he notices Zorba's lips trembling and pathetically remarks, "We all have to go the same way..." While Zorba moans, weeps, and refuses consolation, Boss falls back on the Myth of Eternal Recurrence and consoles himself that actually the widow died thousands of years ago. Despite his recent experience with the widow, Boss is still a divided personality who stands around intellectualizing uncomfortably in the presence of strong emotions expressed by others. Emotions of revenge or anger over-the widow's death (if they exist at all) are less strong in Boss than his concern for Zorba's safety. His strongest emotion is a need to be peacemaker between Zorba and the widow's murderer. With Boss as the narrator, Kazantzakis no doubt had problems presenting swiftly and compactly in these two chapters the Hogarthian gallery of characters. The point of view throughout the novel remains with the cerebral Boss, but in these chapters his descriptions and musings seem to get inside and look out from another's point of view...as when he imagines Hortense's death from the parrot's point of view, or when he senses the freedom of being old and unworried enough to be able to watch butterflies like Anagnosti does.

Zorba's responses to the death of the widow and "Bouboulina" are a combination of overwhelming grief, defiance, decisive action, storytelling, and fear of aging. And as usual his words and emotions are marvelously concrete and sensuous. For example, one sniff of orange water reminds him of the widow, and he begins lamenting:

> **"How many years it's taken," he muttered, "how many long years for the earth to succeed in making a body like that! You looked at her and said: Ah! if only I were twenty and the whole race of men disappeared from the earth and only that woman remained, and I gave her children! No, not children, real gods they'd be... Whereas now..." (277).**

Zorba's determination to hold God to account for the widow's death is one of those reversals of Christian religious beliefs that Kazantzakis delighted in. No doubt, the exact opposite of a repentant sinner trembling before Almighty God on Judgment Day is the image of mighty Zorba declaring that he'll never forgive God and that God will be ashamed to appear before Zorba in the event that there actually is a Judgment Day. Another example of Zorba's powerful, sensuous concreteness is his response to "Bouboulina's" death. While Boss floats in **metaphysical** realms, while villagers noisily gather for ceremonies, or thieving, Zorba looks wonderingly at "Bouboulina" and thinks: "A bit of earth that was hungry...and laughed, and kissed. A lump of mud that wept human tears. Arid now?... Who the devil brings us onto this earth and who the devil takes us away?" (295).

CHAPTER 24

Zorba and Boss consider many questions about immortality and the purpose of man and matter, until Zaharia interrupts them. After Zaharia dies, Zorba mysteriously alludes to making miracles.

Grub **Imagery**. Throughout the novel, Boss and sometimes Zorba have likened man to a grub - a tiny insect. This **imagery** emphasizes man's smallness, limited powers, and origin from the earth. In Chapter 24 Boss attempts to define "sacred awe" for Zorba by likening man to a grub and the earth to a leaf. The grubs' responses resemble responses of three kinds of men whom Boss later characterizes.

Patterns In The Relationship. During lengthy conversations, Boss will frequently try to instruct Zorba. Sometimes his remarks are condescending; for example, at the end of the grub story, he remarks that Zorba could not understand "when poetry begins." Then Boss does an "about face," berates himself for being a pen-pusher, and admires Zorba for being a "real man." Again and again Boss goes through this pattern of first trying to be critical of Zorba and then unabashedly admiring him. Again and again Boss expounds only to be silenced with the realization either that Zorba's stories are more to the point or that Zorba is the real thing that he - Boss - is only theorizing about. And repeatedly Zorba counterpoints this pattern. First, Zorba listens like a note-taking pupil, then declares abruptly that Boss should tear up his books and really start living again. After declaring either that Boss is too vague or that Zorba is too dumb, Zorba launches into a marvelous story, which usually elicits Boss' response of you're-great-and-I'm-lacking.

As these examples demonstrate, this pattern of responses dramatizes Boss' and Zorba's relationship while they're talking. Even so, for the Western reader not accustomed to this kind of novel, which some critics label "a philosophical novel," the talking may seem too long and the pattern of responses too repetitious - especially in this chapter. After the vivid and compact drama of Chapters 22 and 23, Chapter 24 gets limpingly under way with Zorba's question "Why do people die?" But then Zorba's Rabelaisian escapade with the mad monk Zaharia provides needed comic relief. (For a discussion of Rabelais' and Kazantzakis' humor, see textual analysis of Chapters 16–18.)

Three Kinds Of Men. Many times in earlier chapters Boss has mentioned various types of human responses and has pondered their meaning. In this chapter he speaks as if he has finally come to some definite conclusion and delineates for Zorba three types of men. Boss' description of (1) those who live their own lives, (2) those who concern themselves with the lives of all men, and (3) those who live the life of the entire universe, could well be a description of (1) Zorba, (2) Stavridaki, and (3) Boss, respectively. These types also resemble the three types described in Boss' story about grubs who crawl to the precipice: one grub is dizzy and delirious, a second grub strengthens his heart with the word "God," and a third, a calm, brave grub declares, "I like it." Zorba - the first type of man (or grub) sensuously and passionately lives his life without comforts of religion, political allegiances, or feelings that he is part of a larger evolutionary process. Stavridaki - the second type - appears in Boss' letters and memories to be filled with a sense of duty, with a religious need to deny himself and "save" others; his chiding of Boss for being a pen-pusher is one of the main reasons Boss decides to try mining in Crete. Finally, there is Boss - the third type of man (or grub) - who attempts to live the life of the entire universe. Like Kazantzakis and Bergson, Boss sees man and matter as part of an evolutionary process involved in "the same terrible struggle." Boss' remarks about the life of the universe and "turning matter into spirit" refer to important aspects of Kazantzakis' philosophy (which are discussed in detail in textual analysis of Chapters 4 and 6).

Zorba, Stavridaki, and Boss could also be considered as three aspects of the same personality, three psychological components: Id, Superego, and Ego as discussed by Sigmund Freud. Passionate, lusty Zorba would embody the Id; chiding, duty-bound Stavridaki would embody the Superego, and a case could easily be made for Boss as the Ego. Also, the Monk Zaharia (Ego) has an Id character (Brother Joseph) and a Superego character (God) in his three-faceted personality. Those interested in pursuing further this psychological interpretation should consult selected works of Freud recommended in Dr. Robert Pasotti's Monarch Note on Freud.

CHAPTER 25

After Zorba's scheme for bringing trees down the mountain fails dramatically, Boss and Zorba joyously eat and dance. Later Boss receives a psychic message that Stavridaki is going to die.

Reversal Of Christian Beliefs. Kazantzakis' assertion that man is the savior of God (see textual analysis of Chapter 4) and Zorba's intention to condemn God on Judgment Day (see textual analysis of Chapters 22–23) are two examples of the many times Kazantzakis reverses traditional Christian beliefs. By Chapter 25, when the reader has been led to expect such reversals, Kazantzakis reverses the reversal, and now it is the Holy Virgin of Revenge who is exonerated. Zorba performs a "miracle," which the astonished monks proclaim to be "The Miracle of the Holy Virgin of Revenge." Somehow, after Zorba's "putdowns" of women and his smug "miracle making," it is very fitting that the Virgin's statue sits serenely overviewing the scurrying humanity and noisy havoc created by a tree sent down the mountain side in her name.

Zorba's Influence On Boss. The most dramatic evidence of Zorba's influence on Boss is Boss' response to the cable line's collapse and his demand that Zorba teach him to dance. (See textual analysis of Chapter 6 for the Dionysiac meaning of dance.) Zorba too is deliriously happy: "And now that you, my boy, can dance as well and have learnt my language, what shan't we be able to tell each other!" (323). After this, Boss describes his own awareness of new growth in language ("enlarged heart," for example), which he used earlier to describe Zorba. Quite like Zorba, Boss now because of his joy can't stop to talk. And, after his distressing psychic message about Stavridaki, Boss rushes headlong down the mountain trying (just as Zorba had done after the widow's death) to "deaden...sorrow by fatigue."

The reader has been gradually prepared for Chapter 25, which dramatizes the power and success of Zorba's influence on Boss. However, Chapter 26, the final chapter, shows the reader that although Zorba's influence was lasting, Boss never became a "Zorbatic" person. Boss' refusal in Chapter 26 to see the green stone symbolizes the limits of Zorba's influence.

CHAPTER 26

Zorba and Boss separate. Boss tells briefly what has happened in the years intervening between his life with Zorba and his decision to write about Zorba. The novel concludes with a letter describing Zorba's death.

Time As A **Theme**. Throughout this novel the meaning of time is explored seriously and humorously from many perspectives. Zorba - despite his occasionally expressed worries about being old - is the only character who lives almost entirely in the present. He worries little about the future and does not need a belief or philosophy to make sense of either his life on earth or his hereafter. His past consists of vivid memories, and when he dies, he says, "the whole Zorbatic world will come crashing down." Zorba's nowness provides a striking contrast to some of the static views of time like Nietzsche's Myth of Eternal Recurrence or the monks' belief in a Christian hereafter. Like mechanistic and teleological views of time, Nietzsche's myth emphasizes that everything is, was, and always will be; thus no change is possible because the future is already determined.

Boss expresses belief in this static, mechanistic view when he declares that the widow actually died a thousand years ago, and the young girls now dancing under the tree were actually born centuries before. But in Chapter 26, Boss has obviously given up this static view of time, and like Bergson and Kazantzakis believes in creative evolution. According to this view, time is not static, and change is possible. (See textual analysis of Chapters 2–3 and 4.) Bergson, the philosopher of creative evolution and a powerful influence on Kazantzakis, presents a dynamic concept of time as duration. According to Bergson (and Kazantzakis) it is through intuition not intellect that man experiences duration: "Pure duration is the form which our conscious states assume when our ego lets itself live," when it **refrains** from separating past from present from future and forms instead one organic whole. Duration is the essence of life because life is never a goal completed but is process and perpetual becoming. A student interested in pursuing further Bergson's concept of time and its significance to *Zorba the Greek* might well conclude that Zorba embodies Bergson's definition of "pure duration," that Stavridaki embodies Bergson's concept of memory, and that this entire concept of time is an important key to understanding the meaning and complexity of this novel.

Because he believes in creative evolution and the possibility of change, Boss realizes that the way man struggles and acts now determines the future of both man and God. In Chapter 26 Boss ponders the shadowy, spiritual presence of Stavridaki and wonders if Stavridaki lived long enough "to immortalize what there was to immortalize in him." Boss senses a relationship between Stavridaki's "human time" and Stavridaki's "immortal time," and soon after (when Boss believes Zorba is dying), he decides to immortalize Zorba in a manuscript. Boss' concept of time is also closely related to his concept of the artist's responsibility.

Responsibility Of Creative Artist. Responsibility of the creative artist as presented in Chapter 26 is an important part of Kazantzakis' philosophy - especially his epistemological idealism, views on myth, and concepts of God. (See textual analysis of Chapters 2–6 and 8–9.) *In Report to Greco*, Kazantzakis says the creative artist - if he formulates his "deepest inner presentiments with integrity" - can aid future man to be born "one drop more integrally." Writers and poets especially, continues Kazantzakis, have a "grave duty" to formulate a new myth, a new course for modern man who has lost his equilibrium, his God, and his heroes. By recreating Zorba in a manuscript, Boss is fulfilling his responsibilities to himself, to Zorba, and to Stavridaki. But, most important of all, Boss the artist is speaking to future man about the power and significance of all those Zorbatic qualities which man may lose only at the peril of his continued evolution. Boss' manuscript about Zorba is a testament not only to the importance of Dionysiac Zorba but also to the importance of Apollonian Boss. After all, Zorba would never have written anything - he danced important things he needed to express. Without Boss to immortalize him, Zorba would have been experienced by only the few who knew him during his lifetime.

Critics ask, "Who is the major character in *Zorba the Greek?*" Some answer, "Zorba." Some answer, "Boss." The real answer is: "Both, equally." *Zorba the Greek* is about Zorba and about Zorba's creator. Like Boss' manuscript, this novel is a testament to Zorbas, to artists, and to art works that unite Zorbas and artists.

ZORBA THE GREEK

CHARACTERIZATION

Characters in this novel move in a "weather of myth." With the exception of Zorba, Kazantzakis presents the characters in a two-dimensional form; usually they function as types and symbols rather than as real human beings in three dimensions. Two major characters - primitive, exuberant Zorba and timid, intellectual Boss - are an important aspect of the novel's pervasive dualities. Their activities are illumined by a host of minor characters who often possess humorous names indicative of their characters. Among the minor male characters, Zaharia and Uncle Anagnosti are especially memorable. The minor female characters include the Widow Sourmelina, Dame Hortense ("Bouboulina"), and numerous female types who appear only briefly. Dame Hortense, Zorba's "scow-bottomed siren" is the only woman who is developed to any degree, and even she possesses a two-dimensional, fairy-tale-like quality that is present in all of the novel's characters. Following in alphabetical order is a brief sketch of the characters in *Zorba the Greek*. Readers should consult the textual analysis for more in-depth characterization, especially of Zorba and Boss. In the following list, very minor characters are identified but not discussed.

Anagnosti, Uncle

A respected and wise old Cretan peasant, Uncle Anagnosti appears briefly throughout the novel, pronouncing on the meanings of various situations. His philosophy is that even with luck, life is hard; if he had it to do over, he would drown himself in the sea. The best descriptions of Uncle Anagnosti are in Chapters 5 and 14.

Androulio

The Cretan peasant Androulio is a "dirty old man" type.

Bishop

The delirious bishop who finds relief in listing verbal adornments of the Virgin is meant to be a caricature of Kazantzakis. Also his "three theories" are part of Kazantzakis' **satire** of intellectuals. The bishop appears only in Chapter 18.

Boss (or "boss")

One of the novel's two main characters, the narrator Boss is the polar opposite of Zorba. Quiet, intellectual, and immersed in his manuscript on Buddha, Boss tries to expand his horizons by running a lignite mine with Zorba as foreman. The most outstanding characteristics about Boss are his divided personality and his attempts to heal the division. His language - though very concrete for an intellectual - meanders around in search of answers as he swings back and forth from admiring Buddha to admiring Zorba, from fearing the widow to desiring her, from admiring the man of action to berating himself for being a "pen-pusher." Always he is caught up expressing life's contradictions and paradoxes. Zorba has a profound but limited influence on him, because in the end Boss does not become a "Zorbatic" person. Instead he uses his pen-pushing talents to immortalize Zorba in a novel. In the final chapters of *Zorba the Greek* Boss' function as a creative artist is very important to the meaning of the novel. For further discussion of Boss see textual analysis, especially of Chapters 2–3, 24, and 26.

"Bouboulina."

(See Hortense)

Canavaro

Throughout, the parrot perched over Dame Hortense's bed screeches, "Canavaro, Canavaro!" According to Dame Hortense's story (based on an actual historical incident), Canavaro, who gave her the parrot, was the first name of an Italian Admiral whom she prevented from attacking Crete. The name Canavaro is also used by the misled Zaharia, who thinks that Zorba's name is Canavaro.

Demetrios, The Monk

Demetrios, the debauched, obese monk and owner of the Tanagra figurine, is probably the murderer of the young novice Gavrili.

Dimitri

Several times Zorba mentions his grief over the death of his three-year old son Dimitri.

Hortense, Dame

Affectionately called "Bouboulina" by Zorba, Dame Hortense is based on an historical person, a young French prostitute, who is reputed to have saved Crete from attack (in one of the nineteenth-century Cretan wars of independence). She is often described in nautical terms such as "a ship's figurehead," a "scowbottomed siren," a "frigate," a wrecked "hulk" looking for "a final harbor." She is the only woman in the novel who is developed to any degree and even she possesses a two-dimensional, fairy-tale-like quality present in all the novel's characters. At times, however, the portrayal of Dame Hortense approaches three dimensionality. When she is mourning her lost youth or showing delight in Zorba, she becomes more than a desperate old woman looking for a man, more than an aging prostitute seeking respectability. Descriptions of her relationship with Zorba and her death are hilarious, tender, and painful - all at the same time. Review Chapters 2–3, 11, and 19 for detailed descriptions of Dame Hortense.

Gavrili

He is the "handsome" and "golden-haired" novice who is murdered in the monastery.

Karayannis

In Chapter 12, Boss receives a funny letter from Karayannis, his Greek friend in Africa who professes to hate Greeks and insists that Boss should join him in Africa.

Katerina

"Crazy" Katerina appears once to curse the widow and urge the village men to avenge Pavli's death.

Kondomanolio

Proprietor of "The Modesty Cafe-and-Butcher's Shop" and one of the village elders, Kondomanolio appears briefly in the novel several times.

Kotopouli

She is an actress who is ridiculed in a story told by Sfakianonikoli.

Lenio, Auntie

She and Malamatenia are the rapacious dirge singers who steal from Dame Hortense.

Lola

She is the woman Zorba takes up with in Candia and describes in a letter to Boss.

Lyuba

Years after the lignite mining adventure, Zorba writes Boss that he is enclosing a picture of Lyuba, who later becomes Zorba's widow.

Malamatenia

She and Auntie Lenio are the rapacious dirge singers who steal from Dame Hortense.

Manolakas

Cousin to Pavli, Manolakas - the village constable - appears intermittently throughout the novel. In a fight over the widow, he chews Zorba's ear; later he and Zorba are reconciled. See Chapter 22.

Mavrandoni

A Cretan peasant and one of the village elders, Mavrandoni (father of Pavli) owns the lignite mine, which Boss rents. To avenge Pavli's death, Mavrandoni murders the Widow Sourmelina. See Chapter 22.

Mimiko

As the village "simpleton," Mimiko is usually available to deliver messages and run errands for the widow Sourmelina and others.

Some of his very practical remarks indicate that he is not stupid. The best description of Mimiko is in Chapter 8.

Mother Superior

She is a very minor character who tells Boss about time and eternity in Chapter 15.

Noussa

Russian Noussa is the subject of a long and funny story that Zorba tells in Chapter 8. Of all Zorba's women, she is the most memorable and "Zorbatic."

Old Man

On a trip in the countryside (Chapter 15), Boss converses with an old man, accompanied by his wife and daughter.

Pavli

Because the widow Sourmelina calls him a boy and will not return his love, Pavli drowns himself.

Sfakianonikoli

He is the "wild shepherd" who tells his drinking companions about seeing a theatre performance starring the actress Kotopouli.

Sifakas

Sifakas, the young shepherd, comes into the village once a year for Easter celebrations and is much admired for his vigorous dancing.

Sophinka

She is the subject of one of Zorba's anecdotes.

Sourmelina, The Widow

Although the alluring, musk-odored widow is seldom present in the direct action, she is much talked about. She is an especially important character because of her effect on the men: Pavli drowns himself for love of her, the village men lust after her, and Boss, after a night with her, is inspired finally to end the Buddha manuscript. When she is murdered by Pavli's revengeful father, the entire village watches. She becomes their scapegoat. For descriptions of the widow and her death, review Chapters 8 and 22.

Stavridaki

Boss' friend Stavridaki is away in the Caucasus rescuing his fellow Greeks from the Kurds. Although he is never present in the direct action, he is an important character. Throughout the novel Boss frequently thinks about and corresponds with Stavridaki. The depth of their attachment is dramatized by the psychic warnings that Boss receives about Stavridaki's impending death. For full understanding of Stavridaki, review Chapters 12 and 25 of the novel.

Stephanos, Pappa

Pappa, the village priest, wears a dirty cassock with big pockets to carry various food offerings.

Zaharia

Zorba has great fun humoring this schizophrenic pyromaniac who is sometimes the monk Zaharia, sometimes the naughty Brother Joseph, and sometimes Christ. After his death, Zaharia's body is used by Zorba to execute a prank which the misled monks believe to be "The Miracle of the Holy Virgin of Revenge." The best descriptions of Zaharia are in Chapters 17 and 24.

Zorba

Zorba, the Dionysiac 65-year-old dancer, lover, and story-teller is considered by many to be one of the great characters of modern fiction. Hired to oversee a mine, he is soon instructing his boss in how to celebrate, laugh, chase women, and see everything as if for the first time. There is no doubt that he is the major source of the novel's humor. His stories about his past are riotously funny, his tender-hilarious relationship with "Bouboulina" is unforgettable, and his actions range from the demonic to the comic as he dramatizes the value of folly by taking his "brakes" off at just that point when most sensible people would put their "brakes" on. Even his casual remarks are colorful ("Life is trouble, yes... Death, no"), and his questions, unlike Boss' philosophical and circuitous musings, cut immediately and humorously to the heart of a matter: "How do you expect to get the better of a devil...if you don't turn into a devil-and-a-half yourself?" According to him, "daytime is a man," "night is a woman," and God holds a big sponge and "Flap, Slap" wipes away sins. Zorba is constantly myth-making and explaining such things as how his grandfather went to heaven by bouncing higher and higher in white rubber shoes. In contrast to intellectual Boss (the mind), Zorba (the body) is associated with primitive origins, "bowels of the earth," and dark underground subconscious forces. He is, according to Boss, a "living heart, a large voracious mouth, a great brute soul, not yet severed from mother earth." Zorba's character - especially his energy, passion, folly, irrationality, dancing, acceptance of contradictions, impatience with bourgeois virtues and religion - is generally considered an outstanding example of Nietzsche's influence on Kazantzakis. For further discussion of Zorba's character see textual analysis, particularly of Chapters 4, 6–18, and 24.

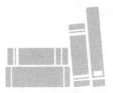

ZORBA THE GREEK

SURVEY OF CRITICISM

Initial Reaction. *Zorba the Greek* (first published in 1946) has been praised in Greece for portraying the exuberant, volatile, Greek temperament and has been equally denounced as vulgar, as an insult to Greek decorum. In 1952, English reviewers of the first English language translation praised the book, for the most part, but admitted that they didn't know quite what to make of it. Later, in 1953, American reviewers gave the book qualified praise, the general response being: "This is a fascinating book despite its departure from what we usually expect of a novel."

"Nothing Like 'Zorba' Has Appeared For Years," says Edmund Fuller (*New York Times Book Review*, April 19, 1953); the novel has vitality, excitement, sweep, and the characters - especially Zorba and the Cretan villagers - are memorable. However, Fuller finds the scholarly narrator somewhat tedious. "Conceptually the novel gets nowhere. It is in the life force of Zorba that its uniqueness rests." Fuller criticizes the philosophy in the novel but, in the total balance, finds much to praise. He exhorts his readers not to miss this book: "It is an unusual experience, for all its contradictions and defeats."

Lack Of Plot And Action. The reviewer for Kirkus (February 15, 1953) praises the humor, pathos, vulgarity, beauty, tragedy and characterization but worries that "the strangeness of rhythm, the lack of surface plot and much direct action will not attract an easy audience." In a similar critical vein, Richard Winston (*New York Herald Tribune Book Review*, April 19, 1953) praises the novel's good humor and originality, but finds that the characters' "anecdotal tradition" has misled Kazantzakis into "blurring the underlying tight construction of his novel." While the effect of characters on plot concerns Winston, the effect of the "plotless" story on the characters concerns the reviewer for Booklist (May 15, 1953). According to this reviewer, the characters, except Zorba, are "more like figures from Greek mythology than real people; the impression is heightened by the episodic construction of this virtually plotless tale."

Some critics find little to praise and imply that *Zorba the Greek* in no way hangs together. "I find it a book of good passages rather than a good book," says Paul Pickrel (*Yale Review*, Summer 1953). Because of its author and prior critical acclaim, Simon Paynter (*Canadian Forum*, February 1953) tries to approach the novel with humility: "Alas, this reviewer's humility proved unequal to the test, and he must report that this is an exasperatingly silly book, alleviated only by Cretan color and one or two fairly effective scenes."

Contrasts Three Ways Of Life. Kimon Friar, translator of Kazantzakis' *The Odyssey: A Modern Sequel*, asks the reader to refocus his "mental eye" in order to find "the symbolic figure entwined in the rude landscape" (*New Republic*, April 27, 1953):

Once the point of view is established, the plan is easily grasped in its magnificent boldness and simplicity, the characters and their action take on symbolic

universality, and the movement becomes that of the shifting anecdote or the erratic exuberance of the picaresque tale.

This is not a realistic story in three dimensions, says Friar; the three main **episodes** (Zorba's affair, the widow's death, and the burning of the monastery) occur on a level similar to fairy tale and legend. Essentially, "the book contrasts three ways of life": (1) Stavros' way of duty and sacrifice, (2) the narrator's withdrawal and inner struggles "to convert matter into spirit," and (3) Zorba's indulgent, joyous, instinctual way.

Fable Of Mind And Body: Deliberately Void Of Plot. The narrator is the mind and Zorba is the body, writes G. D. Painter (*New Statesman and Nation*, September 6, 1952). Neither becomes more like the other, but together these partners bring to the reader a rich and fantastic world. After examining the two main characters in detail, Painter asks: "How can a novel so deliberately void of plot give such an exciting sense of onward movement?" His answer is that Western man has come to view time unnaturally. In *Zorba the Greek* time is changed back "to its reality of moment upon moment."

Poet's Novel. The critic for the *London Times* (*Literary Supplement*, October 3, 1952) begins his review by explaining that Greek novels have little in common with Western fiction: "The Greek novelist prefers to exist in the moment, to express a single vision and to reach towards a philosophical understanding of basic human problems." Thus, *Zorba the Greek* is well integrated, and is in fact "a poet's novel." In it Kazantzakis has created "one of the great characters of modern fiction."

Sainted Rascal. Reviewers love to characterize Zorba and frequently indulge themselves to such an extent that more than half of their reviews consist of lively sketches of the "wild and wily Zorba," the "life force a la Grecque," "current of electricity," "weatherbeaten ruffian," "hawk-eyed primitive," "old codger," "neo-Hellenic Pan," "good and happy man," "Everyman with a Greek accent," "doughty Greek," "unspoiled, great soul," etc. According to one reviewer, Zorba belongs in the "national gallery of sainted rascals" (Unsigned, *The Nation*, May 2, 1953). He is frequently likened to Odysseus, Don Quixote, Panurge, Sinbad, Falstaff and Sancho Panza, and his creator is said to be writing in the tradition of Homer, Cervantes, Celine, Rousseau, Aristophanes, Voltaire, Plautus, and especially in the tradition of Rabelais. One critic finds Zorba so alive and convincing that he criticizes Kazantzakis for unsuccessfully trying to kill off Zorba in a letter. "But Author Kazantzakis reckons without his own talent. He created Zorba, but he cannot kill him" (Unsigned, *Time*, April 20, 1953). Another critic maintains that men like Zorba have always existed: pioneers, warriors, heroes of legends, "enchanted madmen" like Don Quixote. "We have had our share of them in this country, though we are now apt to catch them young and turn them over to the psychiatrist or the reform school" (Harrison Smith, *Saturday Review*, May 30, 1953).

Philosophical Novel. Zorba moves most readers and reviewers. One exception, however, is Sean Callery (*Commonweal*, May 5, 1953) who finds him uninteresting and unbelievable. This is a "philosophical novel," says Callery, and Zorba, like the other characters, is "contrived to illustrate various maxims." Callery finds the tales "tiresome" and repetitive and the philosophy "commonplace and unenlightening." The only thing he can find to praise is the Cretan setting and the lesser characters, who seem to have a potential which Kazantzakis did not develop.

Realism And Kazantzakis. In contrast to Friar, Painter, and some others, Anthony West discusses *Zorba the Greek* as a realistic novel that celebrates life "in a manner that is at once altogether realistic and altogether happy" (*New Yorker*, April 25, 1953). Currently, says West, our Western **realism** is unhappy, and our realistic "heroes" go about beating their breasts and acting like anything but heroes:

> **More than anything else, this idea of the creative arts as a wailing wall to which one goes to get an easement of personal distress gives contemporary writing its "period" flavor; almost every time one opens a book of any intellectual pretensions it is to hear the monotonous shrill scream of a private pain. The spirit in which Kazantzakis writes is wholly alien to this.**

West, like Kimon Friar, compares Kazantzakis with D. H. Lawrence and finds their writing "alive in the same way"; Lawrence, however, could not "risk being funny," and one of the marvelous things about *Zorba the Greek* is its "rich vein of humor."

Novel Of The Year. At the end of the year, *Time* magazine chose *Zorba the Greek* as "the richest, most exuberant novel of the year." Zorba, himself, was welcomed for his belief that it is good to be alive: "By comparison, the chest-beating hero of Saul Bellow's *The Adventures of Augie March* was a neurotic wise guy - though Augie did better than Zorba in the bookstores."

Later Criticism. During the next eleven years after the translation of *Zorba the Greek*, seven more novels and various works of non-fiction by Kazantzakis were translated into English and other languages. Reviewers frequently compare the characters of subsequent novels with characters in *Zorba the Greek*. Now that they have an array of Kazantzakis' characters, reviewers have been discovering ways in which Zorba is or is not typical of Kazantzakis' hero types. Philip Deane, reviewing *Report to Greco*, delineates Kazantzakis' "two standard" characters - the "hero-warrior" and the "hero-martyr" (*The New Republic*, October 2, 1965). According to Deane, Zorba is a hero-warrior and Boss is a hero-martyr.

In the middle sixties, two events brought special attention to *Zorba the Greek* - the publication of Kazantzakis' spiritual autobiography, *Report to Greco*, and the release of the film *Zorba*. Reviewers of *Report to Greco* mentioned Zorba because the biography recounts Kazantzakis' meeting of Giorghos Zorba, the real Greek who inspired the fictional Alexis Zorba. And concerning the effect of Cacoyannis' film, *Zorba*, Joseph Blenkinsopp says that it "boosted the sales of the novels and worked wonders for Greek restaurateurs" (*Commonweal*, February 26, 1971). By 1969, when the musical play based on the novel (directed by Harold Prince) appeared, even the theologians had discovered *Zorba the Greek*; such people as John Robinson, Harvey Cox, and Sam Keen were quoting from the novel. Scholars, too, were turning their attention to *Zorba the Greek* and were discovering the influences of Henri Bergson, Friedrich Nietzsche, and others on Kazantzakis.

Nietzsche's Influence. Andreas K. Poulakidas and Peter Bien discuss the considerable influence of Friedrich Nietzsche on Kazantzakis. As an influence on *Zorba the Greek*, Poulakidas emphasizes *Thus Spake Zarathustra* by Nietzsche and Bien emphasizes Nietzsche's *The Birth of Tragedy*. According to Poulakidas, Zarathustra was a split personality who could not be the "overman" ("ubermensch") he envisioned. Kazantzakis realizes what Nietzsche failed to accomplish, and so "he operates on Zarathustra, separating his two selves and making both integral, functional, and human in *Zorba the Greek*." Thus both Zorba and the Boss "fulfill Nietzsche's *Zarathustra*, both in philosophy and in character."

According to Bien, we should not be misled by the seeming gaiety and spontaneity of *Zorba the Greek*. The novel is a well-constructed "philosophic parable" about the clash and eventual fusion of Eastern and Western forces, "which both Nietzsche and Kazantzakis see as so singularly and perennially Greek." To explain this clash and fusion, Bien uses abstract terminology that Nietzsche employed in defining Apollonian and Dionysian aspects of classical art ("strong pessimism" and "weak pessimism," which are in opposition to "optimism"). Using Nietzschean terminology, Bien concludes that *Zorba the Greek* is a "parable of Dionysiac knowledge, Dionysiac wisdom, made concrete through Apollonian artifice."

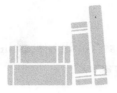

ZORBA THE GREEK

Question: How might Zorba fare in our world? What might he be doing to make a living?

Answer: A good case could be made both for and against the possibility of Zorba's surviving (or even being born) in a Western technological civilization. Chances are, if Zorba were alive in our society, he would be in prison or maybe hitchhiking about taking on odd jobs. According to critic Harrison Smith, men like Zorba have always existed: pioneers, warriors, heroes of legend, "enchanted madmen" like Don Quixote. "We have had our share of them in this country, though we are now apt to catch them young and turn them over to the psychiatrist or the reform school" (Saturday Review, May 30, 1953). In formulating your own answer, you might want to consider the following questions. To what extent is Zorba essentially Greek? Is there a relation between the meaning of dance to Zorba and the meaning of dance to current youth? To what extent are Zorba's Dionysiac qualities (see textual analysis of Chapter 6) expressed in our society, at the Esalen Institute, on college campuses, at rock festivals?

Question: Compare and contrast the literary techniques and style of *Zorba The Greek* with the literary techniques and style in the passage quoted below. This quotation from the "Epilogue" of Kazantzakis' spiritual autobiography, *Report To Greco*, was written not long before Kazantzakis died of complications resulting from leukemia; here he acknowledges that the end of his life is near.

Now the twilight cast its haze upon the hilltops. The shadows have lengthened, the air has filled with the dead. The battle is drawing to a close. Did I win or lose? The only thing I know is this: I am full of wounds and still standing on my feet.

Answer: This passage is very typical of many passages in *Zorba the Greek* (written originally in demotic Greek). The description of the setting as reflecting a mood of the speaker, the abundance of sensuous images, the metaphoric reference to life as a battle, the terse question and concretely expressed but noncommittal answer - all these elements of style and literary techniques are present in *Zorba the Greek*.

Question: Throughout the novel various characters refer to a "Palikari." Define "Palikari" and discuss the significance of this term in *Zorba The Greek*.

Answer: "Palikari" refers to a soldier of the Greek militia in the war of independence (1821–1828) against Turkey. As used by various characters in this novel, "Palikari" is an especially reverential term meaning "He is a real hero." According to Zorba, "My father was a real Palikari... He was one of those ancient Greeks they always talk about. When he shook your hand he nearly crushed your bones to pulp" (336). From the way in which Zorba and others use the word "Palikari" the reader is able to sense that not only is a "Palikari" immediately recognized and universally admired, but alas, he is a dying breed. This sense - that such widely accepted heroes exist no longer - is related to Kazantzakis' **theme** about the bankruptcy of Western civilization and the need for heroes and myths that are meaningful to the modern man.

Question: What attitude toward women is expressed in the following quotation from Kazantzakis' spiritual autobiography, *Report To Greco*? Are similar attitudes found in *Zorba The Greek*?

> **But we did not allow women, even the dearest, to lead us astray. We did not follow their flower-strewn road, we took them with us. No, we did not take them, the dauntless companions followed our ascents of their own free will.**

Answer: Trying to figure out Kazantzakis' attitude toward women as expressed in his fiction, philosophy, and letters is a perplexing task. The first two sentences of this quotation are probably more emotionally honest than the third sentence. However, Kazantzakis was both the man who chose fruitful relationships with sensitive, intelligent women and the man who filled *Zorba the Greek* and other works with ridiculous women and constant remarks about woman's inferiority. In his fiction and philosophy man is usually spirit and woman is flesh; woman almost always equals sexual enticement and domesticity, both of which man must avoid if he is to evolve into a higher being and fulfill his purpose. But - as evident in the above quotation - Kazantzakis frequently tries to acknowledge women's strengths and individuality. After calling woman a plaything or divine incarnation of "all the adverse powers," for example, he will then exactly reverse himself and call women warriors and invaluable strugglers. In the quotation he first refers to women in "flower-strewn paths" who would lead men astray, and then he says, "No," women were in fact "dauntless companions."

The general attitude toward women in *Zorba the Greek* is much more of the "flower-strewn" variety than the "dauntless companion" variety. One critic suggests that on reading this novel, a feminist might have a "falling fit." Without being an ardent feminist, any reader could easily find numerous "putdowns" of women in every chapter. Chapter 6 alone might dismay even a woman who thinks "a woman's place is in the home." The main source of chauvinistic remarks in the novel is Zorba. According to him, marriage is "the Great Folly," and women are "the everlasting business." Women spend their time setting "traps for men who are always big enough fools to fall into the trap." Furthermore, women are "weak," "incomprehensible," the source of great temporary pleasure. Because woman's "not human," men shouldn't "bear her any grudge," says Zorba.

Question: Some critics maintain that the novel should end where the movie ends - with wild dancing on the beach after the cable collapses. If the novel ended in Chapter 25, what dimensions of meaning would be omitted? Why, do you think, have some critics suggested this ending for the novel?

Answer: Critics who want the novel to end where the movie ends no doubt consider Zorba the major character and Boss rather colorless and boring. Wild dancing near collapsed cable lines, Theodorakas' music...a close-up shot, then a wide angle shot - all this before the final screen credits makes a dramatic ending for a movie. But in the novel, such an ending would lessen the importance of Boss' role because the reader would never know about Boss' manuscript on Zorba. Such an ending (eliminating Chapter 26 and parts of 25) would lessen the significance of Kazantzakis' **theme** about responsibility of creative artists. Responsibility of the creative artist as presented in Chapter 26 is an important part of Kazantzakis' philosophy: the creative artist - if he formulates his "deepest inner presentiments with integrity" - can aid future man to be born "one drop more integrally (Report to Greco). Writers and poets especially, continues Kazantzakis, have a "grave duty" to formulate a new myth, a new course for modern man who has lost his equilibrium, his God, and his heroes. By recreating Zorba in a manuscript, Boss is fulfilling his responsibilities to himself, to Zorba, and to Stavridaki.

But, most important of all, Boss the artist is speaking to future man about the power and significance of all those Zorbatic qualities which man may lose only at the peril of his continued evolution. Boss' manuscript about Zorba is a testament not only to the importance of Dionysiac Zorba but also to the importance of Apollonian Boss. After all, Zorba would never have written anything - he danced important things he needed to express. Without Boss to immortalize him, Zorba would have been experienced by only the few who knew him during his lifetime.

ZORBA THE GREEK

TOPICS FOR RESEARCH AND CRITICISM

....

1. The Meaning of Dance Today and in *Zorba the Greek*

2. Kazantzakis' and Rabelais' Humor: A Comparison and Contrast

3. A Woman's Reactions to the Man's World of *Zorba the Greek*

4. Death and Decay as Portrayed in *Zorba the Greek* and in Other Modern, Western Novels

5. Zorba and Boss: A Fable of Body and Mind

6. Zorba, Boss, and Stavridaki: *Three Different Ways of Life*

7. Nikos Kazantzakis and Herbert Marcuse on "The Synthesis"

8. Kazantzakis' View of Art and T.S. Eliot's "Objective Correlative"

24. Kazantzakis' View of Suffering in *Zorba the Greek*

25. Kazantzakis and Dostoevsky: *Two Different Views on the Meaning of Suffering*

26. Nikos Kazantzakis as portrayed in *Nikos Kazantzakis: A Biography Based on his Letters* by Helen Kazantzakis

27. Saul Bellow's Augie March and Nikos Kazantzakis' *Zorba: Two Very Different Heroes*

28. Demotic Greek and Kazantzakis' Style in *Zorba the Greek*

29. Kazantzakis' View of Women in *Zorba the Greek, The Last Temptation of Christ,* and *Nikos Kazantzakis: A Biography Based on His Letters*

30. *Zorba* and *Don Quixote*: Two Enchanted Madmen

BIBLIOGRAPHY

SELECTED WORKS BY KAZANTZAKIS

Fiction

The Fratricides. Translated from Greek by Athena Gianakas Dallas. New York: Simon & Schuster, 1964 (available in paperback, Simon & Schuster).

Freedom or Death. Translated from Greek by Jonathan Griffin. Preface by A. Den Doolaard. New York: Simon & Schuster, 1956 (available in paperback, Simon & Schuster and Ballantine Books, Inc.) Originally titled *Captain Michalis* in Greek, translated as *Freedom and Death* (1954) in England and as Freedom or Death (1956) in U.S.

The Greek Passion. Translated from Greek by Jonathan Griffin. New York: Simon & Schuster, 1954 (available in paperback, Simon & Schuster and Ballantine Books, Inc.). Published in England under the title *Christ Recrucified.* Novel was made into French film, "He Who Must Die."

The Last Temptation of Christ. Translated from Greek by P. A. Bien. New York: Simon & Schuster, 1960 (available in paperback, Simon & Schuster). First published in 1955.

The Rock Garden. Translated from French by Richard Howard. Passages from *The Saviors of God: Spiritual Exercises* translated by Kimon Friar. New York: Simon & Schuster, 1963 (available in paperback, Simon & Schuster).

Saint Francis. Translated from Greek by P. A. Bien. New York: Simon & Schuster, 1962 (available in paperback, Simon & Schuster and Ballantine Books, Inc.).

Toda Raba. Translated from French by Amy Mims. New York: Simon & Schuster, 1964. Originally published in 1934.

Zorba the Greek. Translated from Greek by Carl Wildman. New York: Simon & Schuster, 1953 (available in paperback, Ballantine Books, Inc.) Originally published in 1946. Published 1952 in England by Scott-Kilvert with Introduction by John Lehmann.

Poetry

The Odyssey: A Modern Sequel. Translation into English verse, Introduction, Synopsis, and Notes by Kimon Friar. Illustrated by Ghika. New York: Simon & Schuster, 1958 (available in paperback, Simon & Schuster). Originally published in 1938.

Philosophy

Saviors of God: Spiritual Exercises. Translated from Greek with an Introduction by Kimon Friar. New York: Simon & Schuster, 1960 (available in paperback, Simon & Schuster). Originally published in 1928 as *Salvatores Dei.*

Nonfiction

England: A Travel Journal. Translated from Greek. New York: Simon & Schuster, 1966.

Japan, China. Translated from Greek by George C. Pappageotes. Epilogue by Helen Kazantzakis. New York: Simon & Schuster, 1963.

Journey to the Morea. Translated from Greek by F. A. Reed. Photography by Alexander Artemakis. New York: Simon & Schuster, 1965.

Report to Greco. Translated from Greek by P. A. Bien. New York: Simon & Schuster, 1965.

Spain. Translated from Greek by Amy Mims. New York: Simon & Schuster, 1963.

Drama

Three Plays. Translated from Greek by Athena Gianakas Dallas. New York: Simon & Schuster, 1969.

SELECTED WRITINGS ABOUT KAZANTZAKIS AND HIS WORKS

Banks, Arthur C. and Finley C. Campbell. "Vision of the Negro in the Kazantzakian Universe." *Phylon* 25 (Fall 1964), pp. 254–262.

In three works (*The Odyssey: A Modern Sequel, The Last Temptation of Christ, and The Greek Passion*), the Negro "is not only the sordid purveyor of passionate sensualism, he is also a dynamic force... [He] projects the paradoxical ambivalence of flesh and spirit."

Bien, Peter. "The Demoticism of Kazantzakis" in *Modern Greek Writers*. Edited by Edmund Keeley and Peter Bien (pp. 146–169). New Jersey: Princeton University Press. 1972.

Describes the role of "the language question" in Kazantzakis' career and how in the novels "his demoticism had finally found its proper artistic embodiment."

————. *Kazantzakis and the Linguistic Revolution in Greek Literature*. New Jersey: Princeton University Press, 1972.

Detailed and learned discussion of "the language question" in Greece from ancient times to the time of Kazantzakis. Explains Kazantzakis' use of demotic Greek and his role in the linguistic revolution.

————. "Nikos Kazantzakis" in *The Politics of Twentieth-Century Novelists*. Edited by George A. Panichas (pp. 137–159). Foreword by John W. Aldridge. New York: Hawthorn Books, Inc., 1971.

Bien stresses the "essential totality of Kazantzakis" and his "circumstantial" relation to politics: "Kazantzakis, like Odysseus, took the road of active political participation in order to arrive at a self-knowledge, meaningfulness and sanctification." Bien discusses in detail Kazantzakis' views on freedom and his theory of history.

————. "A Note on the Author and His Use of Language" in *The Last Temptation of Christ* (pp. 497–505). New York: Simon & Schuster, 1960.

Brief biography of Kazantzakis. Very good discussion of demotic Greek and why Kazantzakis used it. "Demotic Greek shows us a race to whom imagination and audacity come before precision and efficiency."

————. "*Zorba the Greek*, Nietzsche, and the Perennial Greek Predicament." *Antioch Review* 25 (Spring 1965), pp. 147–163.

Considers Nietzsche's *The Birth of Tragedy* to be the model for *Zorba the Greek*. Interprets *Zorba the Greek* as a "philosophic parable" about the clash and eventual fusion of Eastern and Western Forces, "which both Nietzsche and Kazantzakis see as so singularly and perennially Greek."

Blenkinsopp, Joseph. "My Entire Soul is a Cry: The Religious Passion of Nikos Kazantzakis." *Commonweal* 93 (February 26, 1971), pp. 514–518.

Examines Kazantzakis' "considerable" influence in America and says an explanation of this influence may "best be looked for in *Zorba the Greek*." Emphasizes the influence of Nietzsche and Bergson on Kazantzakis.

Bloomfield, Paul. *Manchester Guardian* (September 19, 1952). p. 4.

Reviews *Zorba the Greek*.

Booklist. 49 (May 15, 1953), p. 304. Unsigned. Reviews *Zorba the Greek*. "The characters, with the exception of Zorba, seem more like figures from Greek mythology than real people."

Bulletin of Bibliography and Magazine Notes. "Kazantzakis in America; A Bibliography of Translations and Comment." 25 (September 1968), pp. 166–170.

Callery, Sean. "Dialogues." *Commonweal* 58 (May 8, 1953). Reviews *Zorba the Greek*. Considers the prose "labored," the tales "tiresome," and the philosophy "commonplace and unenlightening."

Chilson, Richard W. "The Christ of Nikos Kazantzakis." *Thought* 47 (Spring 1972), pp. 69–89.

Says the Christ of Kazantzakis' works is not in the Christian tradition and can only be understood in terms of Kazantzakis' own life and thought. Good discussion of the dualisms within Kazantzakis and his works.

Ciardi, John. "The Seven Stages of the Soul." *Saturday Review* 41 (December 13, 1958), p. 17.

Reviews *The Odyssey: A Modern Sequel* as an allegory of the soul: this "is not a book of the year, nor a book of the decade, but a monument of the age."

Clements, Robert J. "European Literary Scene." *Saturday Review* 52 (June 7, 1969), p. 28.

Describes the desecration of Kazantzakis' tomb in Crete.

Davenport, Guy. "The Cretan Glance." *National Review* 17 (October 19, 1965), pp. 937–938.

Reviews and compares works by Kazantzakis (*Report to Greco* and *The Fratricides*) and by Pandelis Prevelakis (*The Sun of Death*). Good discussion of Kazantzakis' hero types.

Deane, Philip. "Old Man From Crete." *New Republic* 153 (October 2, 1965), pp. 26–27.

Reviews *Report to Greco*. Outlines two of Kazantzakis' standard characters the "hero-warrior" and the "hero-martyr."

Decavalles, Andonis and Louis Coxe. "Two views of Kazantzakis." *Poetry* 95 (December 1959), pp. 175–181. Two reviews of *The Odyssey: A Modern Sequel*. Decavalles considers it "the greatest long poem of our time, a colossal achievement." Coxe considers it a "romantic failure"; some of his criticisms are similar to those of *Zorba the Greek*.

Doulis, Tom. "Kazantzakis and the Meaning of Suffering." *Northwest Review* VI (1963).

Includes a discussion of Kazantzakis as a novelist who rejects Western traditions of novel writing.

Friar, Kimon. "Introduction" to *The Odyssey: A Modern Sequel.* New York: Simon & Schuster, 1958.

Sections II and III (pages xii–xxvi) contain an excellent discussion of Kazantzakis' philosophy with specific information about the influence of Bergson and Nietzsche. Friar also clarifies "two aspects of Kazantzakis' thought, which have been most misrepresented" - his attitude toward despair and his definition of God.

_____. "The Kazantzakis Report." *Saturday Review* 48 (August 14, 1965), p. 34.

Reviews *Report to Greco* as a key to all other works by Kazantzakis.

_____. "A Minor Masterpiece." *New Republic* 128 (April 27, 1953), pp. 20–21.

Reviews *Zorba the Greek.* "It must be read and enjoyed on the level of realistic symbolism...Rousseau and Rabelais are its godfathers."

_____. "The Odyssey of Nikos Kazantzakis." *Saturday Review* 40 (November 30, 1957), pp. 13, 36.

Brief biographical review and reminiscences on occasion of Kazantzakis' death.

_____. "The Spiritual Exercises of Nikos Kazantzakis." Introduction to *The Saviors of God: Spiritual Exercises* (pp. 3–40). New York: Simon & Schuster, 1960.

Interwoven with biographical information is a lengthy discussion of Kazantzakis' philosophy. Contains important references to *Zorba the Greek.*

Fuller, Edmund. "The Long Way to Gethsemane." *Saturday Review* 43 (August 6, 1960), pp. 15–16.

Reviews *The Last Temptation of Christ*. Contains a note by K. Friar comparing Kazantzakis with D. H. Lawrence.

_____. "The Wild and Wily Zorba." *New York Times Book Review* (April 19, 1953) pp. 4–5.

Reviews *Zorba the Greek*. "Conceptually the novel gets nowhere. It is in the life force of Zorba himself that its uniqueness rests."

Kazantzakis, Helen. *Nikos Kazantzakis: A Biography Based on his Letters*. Translated from Greek by Amy Mims. New York: Simon & Schuster, 1968.

Important book based on an outline found among Kazantzakis' papers after his death. Contains excerpts from Kazantzakis' letters and journals, interspersed with commentary by his wife. Covers period from 1923 until his death in 1957.

Kirkus. "Review of *Zorba the Greek*." 21 (February 15, 1953), p. 130. Unsigned.

Praises the novel, but asserts that it "will not attract an easy audience though it is sure to command a discerning public."

Maurer, Robert. "Fiction." *Saturday Review* 53 (February 21, 1970), pp. 42–43.

Reviews *Three Plays*. Discusses Kazantzakis as a dramatist and explains why his plays probably would not be appreciated today in America.

Moore, Everett T. "A City In Torment Over Kazantzakis." *ALA Bulletin* 57 (April 1963), pp. 305–306.

Describes the attempt of some clergymen and their supporters to remove *The Last Temptation of Christ* from several libraries in Southern California.

The Nation. "Sainted Rascal." 176 (May 2, 1953). p. 380. Unsigned.

Reviews *Zorba the Greek.* "The Book...accepts on a grand scale the reader's willingness to explore superstition, hope, inanition, action, love, venality, and finally death and decay."

Painter, G. D. *New Statesman and Nation* 44 (September 6, 1952), p. 271.

Reviews *Zorba the Greek* and asks, "How can a novel so deliberately void of plot, give such an exciting sense of onward movement?"

Paynter, Simon. *Canadian Forum* 32 (February 1953), p. 262.

One of the most negative reviews of *Zorba the Greek.* "This is an exasperatingly silly book, alleviated only by Cretan color and one or two fairly effective scenes."

Pickrel, Paul. "Outstanding Novels." *Yale Review* 42 (Summer 1953), p. xvi.

Reviews *Zorba the Greek.* "I find it a book of good passages rather than a good book."

Poulakidas, Andreas K. "Dostoevsky, Kazantzakis' *Unacknowledged Mentor.*" *Comparative Literature* 21 (Fall 1969), pp. 307–318.

The author believes that without the influence of Dostoevsky and Russian literature, Kazantzakis "would probably have evolved as a novelist of Western culture." Stresses the two novelists' similarities in types of fictional characters, emphases on love, attitudes toward intellectuals, and views on socialism and religion.

_____. "Kazantzakis' *Zorba the Greek* and Nietzsche's *Thus Spoke Zarathustra.*" *Philological Quarterly* 49 (April 1970), pp. 234–244.

Traces many similarities between *Zorba the Greek* and *Thus Spoke Zarathustra.* "Both of Kazantzakis' characters (Zorba and the Boss) are real entities that fulfill Nietzsche's *Zarathustra*, both in philosophy and in character."

Prevelakis, Pandelis. *Nikos Kazantzakis and his Odyssey: A Study of the Poet and the Poem.* Translated from Greek by Philip Sherrard. Preface by Kimon Friar. New York: Simon & Schuster, 1961.

A lifelong friend and fellow Cretan, Prevelakis provides an important study of the poem and an important - though not comprehensive - account of Kazantzakis' life in relation to his **epic** poem.

Riley, Frank. "A Cross in Heraklion." *Saturday Review* 50 (October 14, 1967), pp. 47–48, 51, 95.

A reporter visits the hometown and grave of Kazantzakis ten years after his death. Interesting account of Kazantzakis' funeral service attended by 50,000 Cretans.

Smith, Harrison. "Attic Mustard." *Saturday Review* 36 (May 30, 1953), p. 16.

Reviews *Zorba the Greek* - "a strange journey into a haunting, wild, and poetical conception of life."

Stein, Joseph. *Zorba.* Book by Joseph Stein. Music by John Kander. Lyrics by Fred Ebb. Adapted from *Zorba the Greek* by Nikos Kazantzakis. Originally produced and directed on Broadway by Harold Prince. New York: Random House, 1969.

Sullivan, Richard. *Review. Chicago Sunday Tribune* (May 31, 1953), p. 8.

Reviews *Zorba the Greek*.

Time. "Last Testament." 86 (August 13, 1965), pp. 77–78. Unsigned.

Reviews *Report to Greco* - "this awkward, graceless but powerful personal testament." Emphasizes the influence of the real Zorba.

_____. "Life Force a la Grecque." 61 (April 20, 1953) pp. 122, 124, 126. Unsigned.

Reviews *Zorba the Greek*. Considers the novel "nearly plotless but never pointless."

_____. "Lycovrissi Parable." 63 (January 11, 1954), p. 84. Unsigned. Reviews *The Greek Passion*. "The hero of his *Zorba the Greek* was a neo-Hellenic Pan who seemed to have goat-footed his way straight out of pagan mythology."

_____. "The Year in Books." 62 (December 21, 1953), p. 94. Unsigned.

Reviews the best books for 1953: *Zorba the Greek* is "the richest, most exuberant novel of the year."

Times, London, Literary supplement. "Greek Fire." (October 3, 1952), p. 641. Unsigned.

Reviews *Zorba the Greek*. Considers it "a poet's novel."

Twentieth Century Authors. Edited by Stanley Jasspon Kunitz (1st Supplement, pp. 514–515). New York: H. W. Wilson Co., 1955.

Contains a biographical sketch of Kazantzakis and a summary of critical response to *Zorba the Greek* and *The Greek Passion*.

Walsh, Chad. "Soul's Laureate." *Saturday Review* 43 (July 23, 1960), pp. 36–37.

Reviews *The Saviors of God: Spiritual Exercises*. Delineates "two poles" in Kazantzakis' "religious sensibility."

West, Anthony. "Happy and Happy-Go-Lucky." *New Yorker* 29 (April 25, 1953), pp. 114, 117.

Reviews *Zorba the Greek*. Considers Kazantzakis a realist whose spirit is alien to contemporary views of the "creative arts as a wailing wall."

Wilson, Colin. "Nikos Kazantzakis" from *The Strength to Dream: Literature and the Imagination*. Boston: Houghton Mifflin, Co., 1962.

General discussion of the major works. Compares and contrasts Kazantzakis with Shaw, Dostoevsky, and Yeats. "The truth is that Kazantzakis was a man of the nineteenth century..."

Winston, Richard. *New York Herald Tribune Book Review* (April 199, 1953), p. 3.

Reviews *Zorba the Greek*. Praises the novel for humor, originality and invention, but the "anecdotal tradition has lured the author into blurring the underlying tight construction of his novel."

SELECTED WORKS PROVIDING PHILOSOPHICAL AND LITERARY BACKGROUND

Bergson, Henri. *Creative Evolution*. Translated from French by Arthur Mitchell. Foreword by Irwin Edman. New York: Random House, 1944.

Durant, Will. *The Story of Philosophy: The Lives and Opinions of the Greatest Philosophers*. New York: Simon & Schuster, 1933.

Keeley, Edmund, and Peter Bien, editors. *Modern Greek Writers*. New Jersey: Princeton University Press, 1972.

Nietzsche, Friedrich. *The Birth of Tragedy and The Genealogy of Morals*. Translated from German by Francis Golffing. New York: Doubleday and Company, 1956.

Russell, Bertrand. *A History of Western Philosophy and Its Connections with Political and Social Circumstances from the Earliest Times to the Present Day*. New York: Simon & Schuster, 1945.